On October 1, 1982, The Walt Disney Company opened its EPCOT Center to the world, heralding changes that would take the Disney property in Florida from a mere theme park to a world-class resort destination. Authors Steve Alcorn and David Green were there, as employees of Disney's WED Imagineering.

Building a Better Mouse tells the tale of the "hundreds of mostly young. mostly bright and all embarrassingly idealistic people" who worked on Epcot, and gives a unique insider's perspective on what it was like to be in the trenches as a Disney Imagineer in the early 1980s, from pixie dusting - when new employees are indoctrinated into all things Disney - through the craziness of the engineering design process, right up until the last frantic dash to opening day. It is a breathtaking, breezy, -ticket ride of a book, required reading for both hard-core Disnevphiles and people interested in the business side of themed entertainment.

Building A Better Mouse

The Story of the Electronic Imagineers Who Designed EPCOT

By Steve Alcorn & David Green

Theme Perks Inc.
Orlando, FL

Sixth Printing, August 2023

Theme Perks Press
www.themeperks.com

ISBN: 9798857773031

Printed in the United States of America

Acknowledgments

Thanks to David Green, who planned the original version of this book with me, and contributed all the sections that sound like they were written by an English major.

Thanks to Glenn Birket for having the foresight to tape record his experiences, and the generosity to share his tapes with me.

Thanks to Sean Patrick Holland for the cover image, taken from his Futureport '82 project. Using Blender and Unreal Engine, Sean is creating a virtual version of Epcot's Futureworld as it was on opening day. For more information, visit https://www.facebook.com/ groups/2715197761926502

And especially thanks to my wife Linda, for dragging me kicking and screaming into this whole, crazy theme park thing. It's been quite a journey.

Steve Alcorn
Orlando, Florida

How This Book Was Written

After Steve Alcorn and David Green finished working for WED Enterprises, both began working on books about their experiences. David, influenced heavily by Hunter S. Thompson's works and Tom Wolfe's "The Right Stuff," wanted to tell a gonzo story about the behind-the-scenes insanity that was EPCOT Center. Steve, with an eye to the future, wanted to record for posterity one of the greatest engineering achievements of the 20th Century.

When David went to work for Steve at Linn Electronics in 1984, they decided to merge their approaches. "Building A Better Mouse" was born, and they worked on it for over a year. Then Linn Electronics went out of business, David went back to college for a second degree, and the book was shelved for nearly 20 years.

In 2007, for EPCOT Center's 25th anniversary, Steve finished the book as a surprise for David.

Along with the recorded transcripts from Glenn Birket, this book was almost entirely written during or shortly after EPCOT was built. No names have been changed, though some may have been obscured. The experiences described herein do not belong to any one person. Some are David's, some are Steve's, and some belong to persons unattributed. Unless otherwise identified, the "I" used here may be a composite, and should not be taken to be any one individual.

Dedication

This book is dedicated to all of the Imagineers who worked on EPCOT and Tokyo Disneyland in the early 1980s. In an era before personal computers and cell phones, they accomplished the not merely difficult, but the truly impossible. Thanks for the memories.

We'll Always Have Paris

I'm sitting in a room on the ground floor of the Airway Tower in Glendale, California, a bright, white building built in Los Angeles-style pseudo-adobe and red tile. Built in the '20s, this three-story "skyscraper" was once the command tower for some long-defunct airport, used in the final scene of the movie "Casablanca."

At the moment, none of that matters to me. I am sitting here, breathing musty air that reeks (I'm sure I can smell it) of doom and angst. I am hostile to the marrow.

Today shows every expectation of becoming one of those dusty, still-life photos that one locks away in one's memory over the years, occasionally, and most often unexpectedly, uncovering in the recesses of the mind to briefly bring a chuckle or a grimace, or simply to fondle the well-worn edges.

It is the fall of 1983. I have just been laid off after working for over three years at WED Enterprises, the engineering company that does the majority of the electronic, mechanical, architectural, electrical, art and prestidigitation for all of Walt Disney's theme parks, from Disneyland in California, to Disney World and EPCOT in Florida to Tokyo Disneyland. Throughout the past year, hundreds of employees have been laid off, but somehow, I am alone in my grief.

During the time I worked for Disney, I fell in love with the company. When I walked into a room, pride radiated from my big, beautiful mouse ears. But yesterday, my ears were amputated with a slip of pink paper and it still hurts like hell.

So here I am, waiting in this beautiful, anachronistic building. Waiting for a job counselor to plot my future career. But what act can they book to follow Disney?

I am neither the first nor the last employee to get the boot, but I still feel surprised and shocked. Figuratively, there's been blood all over the floors of the company since the first mass layoffs of December, 1982. Anybody with half a brain knew it was coming. But somehow it's different when it's your blood.

Those damned ears – they prevent you from thinking clearly.

So here I am, waiting for an appointment with a job counselor, as the frames of my life roll before my eyes in slow sepia flashbacks, fading from scene to scene. Thinking about Disneyland, Disney World and Tokyo Disneyland. Thinking about mice, ducks and talking animals. Thinking about a man with a mustache and a mouse with a bow tie. But most of all, thinking about EPCOT[1] – the Experimental Prototype Community of Tomorrow. Walt's greatest dream they billed it, I guess it was a dream for a lot of us.

I was hired by Disney to help create EPCOT, as were hundreds of other young, mostly bright and all embarrassingly idealistic people. I believed in the dream, the company, and most of all, the ideal – that a Disney employee had one goal: to make as many other people happy as humanly possible.

But the ideal had failed for me, because the company had failed us – they were laying us off.

Perhaps WED knew that after a project the magnitude of EPCOT, no one could be happy with regular work again. Maybe they knew that if they couldn't provide us with the addictive rush of a deadline, it was foolish to keep our hopes alive with a methadone program of busy work. The company was forcing us to quit cold turkey.

Like reluctant missionaries, Disney was cutting us loose by the thousands to spread and preach the gospel of EPCOT. A mad plan, but in my state of cognitive dissonance, it all made sense. The

---

[1] EPCOT Center was renamed Epcot in the 1990s.

company was doing this to make us happy, or else I'd been fooled for three years and so had all the other Disney employees who had worked on EPCOT.

My job counselor arrives.

As we walk through the empty halls to her office, I think about this building just a year ago, bustling with dozens of engineers, technicians, secretaries, clerks, designers and draftsmen. Now, it is almost deserted. The rear offices have been taken over by a group of people from Univance, a placement firm hired by Disney to help people recover from the pain of having their ears amputated.

These Univance people are the cleanup crew. They have to bear the brunt of the ex-employees' pain and hostility, the blank stares, the inevitable "Why me?" The tears.

When we are both seated, my counselor shuffles through my file, leans back comfortably and smiles. "So," she says, "what did you do at EPCOT?"

I close my eyes. Already, it seems so long ago.

Pixie Dust

Walt Disney stands in front of the giant green map of the recently purchased Central Florida property – over 27,000 acres – pointing out the proposed developments. The daring dreamer speaks:

"Here in Florida we have something special we never enjoyed at Disneyland – the blessing of size. There's enough land here to hold all the ideas and plans we can possibly imagine.

"Here in Florida, of course, there will be another amusement theme park similar in size and many other ways to the one in California. We're now developing a master plan that encompasses the theme park and all the facilities around it that will serve the tourist – hotels, motels, and a variety of recreation activities. In fact, this area alone will be five times the size of Disneyland in California... But the most exciting and by far the most important part of our Florida project – in fact, the heart of everything we'll be doing in Walt Disney World – will be our Experimental Prototype Community of Tomorrow. We call it EPCOT...

"(EPCOT will) take its cue from the new ideas and new technologies that are emerging from the creative centers of American industry. It will be a community of tomorrow that will never be completed, but will always be introducing and testing and demonstrating new materials and systems. And EPCOT will always be a showcase to the world for the ingenuity and imagination of American free enterprise...

"A project like this is so vast in scope it will take the cooperation of many people to make it reality...

"We must have the flexibility in Disney World to keep in pace with tomorrow's world. We must have the freedom to work in cooperation with American industry, and to make decisions based on standards of performance. If we have this kind of freedom, I'm confident we can create a world showcase for American free enterprise that will bring new industry to the state of Florida from all over the country.

"I believe we can build a community here that more people will talk about and come to look at than any other area in the world. I'm sure this Experimental Prototype Community of Tomorrow can influence the future of city living for generations to come."

The lights in the theater came up, to the applause of two dozen new-hires. This film, created in 1966, was the last that Walt Disney ever made. Now, thirteen years later, it is being used to "Pixie Dust" new employees: people hired to make those words come true.

Pixie-dusting is the Disney way of cementing employee relations. It starts with employee orientation, when "new-hires" are led through a fantastic journey of the entire Disney dream factory, the places where the secret stuff of Disneyland and Walt Disney World is designed, tested, and built.

As far as many people are concerned, the Disney magic is just that – magic. It has the power to turn the most cynical engineer into a cheerful Jiminy Cricket in a matter of weeks. Forget bombs and aerospace! Be an engineer who makes happy things! And take lower pay for the privilege. Funny thing is, it works.

New-hires become a part of the practitioners of that magic, Imagineers, an elite group. They get to work for the company many of them dreamed of as kids – the makers of Mickey Mouse and castles and Matterhorns that loom tall over orange groves. And the great magic power of Pixie Dust begins to take hold. At the end of their first day, the new-hires receive Mickey Mouse name tags with their first names on them ("Walt wanted this to be a first-name company" – sprinkle, sprinkle).

The first few days after hiring immerse each employee in a constant sprinkling of Pixie Dust, a never-ending flood of company

5

memos, newsletters and benefits including a set of free tickets to Disneyland, just to prove to your family and friends that you are a true practitioner of the secret Disney magic.

Pixie Dust had a strange, intoxicating effect on those who used it, and it took only a few weeks for the most straight-looking, stable person to begin exhibiting the unpredictable behavior of a Pixie Dust addict.

After the EPCOT film, there was a film of Disneyland in the 1950's, then excerpts from movies like "Twenty Thousand Leagues Under the Sea," followed by a videotape of not-yet-released features. Following the theater presentation, the new-hires were led around the Studio backlot, past trailers with stars' names on the doors and soundstages where films like "The Black Hole" were being made. Then a free lunch, and a tour of the Animation Building. There the tour guide explained how the classic animated features were created, and why it's too expensive to do it any more.

A man with little horn-rimmed glasses gave them a quick look at the archives. He let them hold one of the thirty Oscars. Much of the gold was worn off from all the people handling it.

Next into the van, for a trip to Glendale, and the WED and MAPO facilities.

WED[2], which stands for Walter Elias Disney, was created by Walt in 1952, and originally shared the studio lot in Burbank. WED's charter was to create an amusement park that Walt had conceived – Disneyland. At first, WED was very small, but as time passed the company moved to Glendale, and was divided into different disciplines. At the top of the status ladder are the Art Directors, whose job is to imagine the attractions of the future. Artists turn these concepts into storyboards. Their drawings are then used to create a detailed description of virtually every square inch of the ride. Once it has received approval, architectural drawings are created. Set designers create costumes and props. The engineering departments are responsible for designing the vehicles, drive system,

---

[2] WED was renamed Walt Disney Imagineering in 1986.

lighting and projection controls, audio and video systems, and animating the figures. They also must control various special effects, such as fog or fire.

In 1965 a sister company, MAPO (short for Mary Poppins) was formed next to WED to do the fabrication of WED's designs.

Walt Disney died on December 15, 1966. His final legacy was the conception of a massive development in Central Florida. After his death, his dreams and ideas would be carried on by WED, particularly the art directors who had worked with him.

With the coming of the mammoth "Florida Project" in 1971 WED's size was increased to handle the task of simultaneously designing and installing dozens of new attractions at a park on the other side of the country. The 27,000 acres that WED reshaped into Walt Disney World in Central Florida at a cost of $300 million comprised the largest privately funded construction project of all time – building 44 miles of canals, moving 9 million cubic yards of earth, digging a lagoon from swampland and using the debris to form a platform for the Magic Kingdom. Also, luxury hotels, golf resorts, shopping villages, campgrounds, and transportation systems including a monorail. There were 87 subcontractors.

And when all was said and done, there was nothing left for all those extra people at WED to do. So they were laid off.

By the end of the 1970's, WED had been reduced to close to its former size. Yet now there was talk of the other part of Walt's legacy, his Experimental Prototype Community of Tomorrow. Budgeted at $400 million (but destined for $1.2 billion), it was to be the crown jewel of the "Florida Project".

EPCOT was originally planned as a sort of Utopian Disneyland – a futuristic showcase of America's best – a place where real families would live and work beneath a Plexiglas dome, under the scrutiny of all Middle America. EPCOT was to be a giant, living laboratory where the biggest and finest American institutions could peddle instant 2001; lifestyles copied right out of 1950's Mom-and-apple-pie science fiction. A daring, glittering, yet somehow naive dream from America's most daring, glittering, naive dreamer.

Somehow, it would work. No Disney dream has ever failed.

But after the death of the daring dreamer the corporate hierarchy paused to take note of the naive. Namely, who would buy it? What kind of family wants their home to be part of a great chrome-and-plastic world's fair, constantly under the gaze of all Middle America?

It was too much of a corporate risk. Even too great for a company that had made its reputation as a taker of corporate risks. So the dream of EPCOT the corporate risk was replaced by the reality of EPCOT Center the corporate compromise, glittering, naive, but somehow not quite as daring a showcase from the disciples of the daring dreamer.

And yet, something of a spark from the original EPCOT survived. In the midst of central Florida, a few miles from Orlando, a new world was growing. Directing the project were a new crop of Imagineers, a group of mostly young, mostly inexperienced engineers who had been, as any veteran Disney employee could tell, thoroughly Pixie-dusted.

* * *

By the middle of 1981, MAPO, the manufacturing area next to WED, was a beehive of activity. MAPO was housed in two large warehouses. The Airway Building was so named because it was located on the site of the runway of the extinct Glendale Airport. It was used for heavy manufacturing, usually involving large pieces of metal cut and welded to form vehicle chassis or fiberglass pieces used to form the bodies.

The other MAPO building, located adjacent to the WED Building was used for most other work. An electrical shop upstairs and downstairs fabricated the electronic equipment designed by the electronics department. There, 19-inch racks or weather-tight metal boxes were machined, parts mounted, point-to-point wiring done, and circuit boards assembled. After a cursory test, the items were then packed and shipped.

This building also housed the area where audio animatronic figures were machined and assembled, joint-by-joint and limb-by-limb. Plastics manufacturing produced anything from a hand to tree leaves. Pelican Alley, so named because it was originally used for building animated birds, was also housed here. Another department of MAPO was called Fur and Feathers.

Throughout MAPO, skilled craftsmen – or new-hires just learning the trade – meticulously applied the detailed finishing touches which distinguish Disney attractions from other theme parks. At one end of the MAPO Building was a loading dock where, for two years, mammoth crates were loaded onto trucks for shipment to Florida. Packed with cartons and crates, they departed several times a week. Some items were so large they were shipped by convoy.

Across the parking lot from the MAPO Building was the WED Building. This building housed the corporate management for WED Enterprises, including the offices of President Carl Bongiorno, Vice-President of Engineering John Zovich, and the Art Directors.

Down one hall were the conference rooms where Walt conceived Disney World, and where the initial EPCOT planning was done. The rear of the building was used for mock-ups of the rides, built to scale. Each scene was about two feet high and four feet wide, and positioned at shoulder height. Walking through them provided a view of each scene as guests would later experience it. In some cases the scenes were such exact replicas of what would later be installed, they created a sense of deja vu.

Another large area was used for Special Effects prototypes – including a complete volcano to be used in the Energy pavilion – and various laser effects. Special Effects was a very large department whose work encompassed electronic, electrical, mechanical, chemical and optical technologies. Most of the Special Effects personnel fell somewhere in between artists and engineers.

Also in the WED Building were the artists who were responsible for the actual look of EPCOT. Their work began with storyboards describing the attractions, including detailed sketches and paintings of each view throughout the park. They also produced detailed drawings of each prop and special effect.

The model shop crafted nearly exact scale replicas of every figure to be built. The models were often extremely detailed. The American Adventure model included moving set pieces to simulate the complex workings of the carriage and lifts.

Located farther north in the San Fernando Valley was the Tujunga Building, a mammoth structure where the largest work was done, and also used as a holding area for crates and parts that could not be stored at MAPO. There, the large set pieces, fabricated from wood, were cut, assembled and painted. Some of the sets were the size of small houses, and required special shipping consideration. Another giant building was used to paint the enormous mural backdrop for the Energy Pavilion ride.

Figure programming took place at Tujunga. As the electronic cabinets used to control the animated figures were completed by the electric shop, they were sent to Tujunga, along with the figures. They were connected, tested and preliminary animation was done to match their movements to the audio track. The animation would later be touched up in the field to allow for variations in the environment and wear and tear on the figures during shipping and installation. Much of the animation programming had to be added in the field because the lighting, lifts, curtains and other major props were not available for programming at Tujunga.

The entire burning town scene from Pirates of the Caribbean at Tokyo Disneyland was set up there for a while. There were also many figures from Country Bear Jamboree... all singing in Japanese.

During their orientation tour, each new employee seemed to share at least one thing: the reverence for the Disney ideal. They were to be the means by which Walt's greatest dream would be achieved. It would mean nearly inhuman work weeks and unprecedented dedication to the task. This is the story of the creation of EPCOT, its engineering, and the people who engineered it.

Welcome to 510

In 1979 WED was just beginning to realize what it was going to take to build EPCOT. Or at least they thought they were.

It takes about three years from the conception of a ride through story boards, rework of the story boards, writing and rewriting the scripts, creating the music, lighting effects, costumes, and engineering the ride, show, and audio systems before the attraction opens to the public. At least it takes that long assuming the full attention of the entire staff is concentrated on only one or two new attractions. Yet WED's aim was to open a theme park with perhaps two dozen attractions in just three years.

Since the opening of Walt Disney World, WED had designed one or two attractions at the same time, but with EPCOT on the drawing boards it was apparent that many more people would be needed for this mammoth task. Instead of one or two pavilions at a time the entire company would be working on two dozen shows and rides. Although preliminary storyboard work was complete, the concepts would change many times over that tightly compressed schedule. Every section of the company would be inundated in 10 times the normal workload. So the ranks of every department began to swell.

* * *

It was obvious from the beginning that it would take some unusual, extraordinary people to survive the massive buildup.

Nowhere was that more true than in department 510, the group of electronic engineers whose responsibility was to make EPCOT work.

With the sophisticated theme of EPCOT, sophisticated equipment would be required to control the shows. The electronic engineering department was divided into three engineering sections to support the development. These sections were show, ride and audio. The show section would be responsible for controlling anything that the guests saw: animated figures, lighting, special effects. The ride section would be responsible for control of the vehicles, drive systems and operator consoles. And the audio section would be responsible for the audio, and later video, at EPCOT: shows, background music, and vehicle sound. In addition, support sections included secretarial staff, wirelisters, designers, drafters, and technicians.

As if this weren't enough, department 510 was also assigned the task of engineering a whole new Fantasyland for Disneyland and – incredibly – another new theme park, Tokyo Disneyland!

***

In January, 1979, Linda Alcorn was fresh out of school, the ink on her diploma still wet and her mind still ingrained with the layout of the UCLA engineering department. She typified the 510 engineers who were to follow. She was, in her own eyes as well as those of her coworkers, a kid. Linda's interest in Disneyland began when she was a very small girl, on her first visit. Perhaps she had always thought of herself as an Imagineer, that unique breed of engineer who works for the Disney organization. As early as age 10 she had constructed a cardboard model of Disneyland on her bedroom floor. So it's not surprising that when she obtained her Bachelor's of Science in Engineering from UCLA, the place she sought employment was WED Enterprises.

WED was at once wonderful and terrifying. Like the many 510 employees who would follow, Linda felt insecurity as much because she knew some of what they expected of her as she did because she didn't know all that would be expected. Linda had never had to deal with panic management, office politics, corporate paperwork, union rules, project approvals, art committees, dog and pony shows, and the whole convoluted manner in which things were accomplished at WED; things that could not be prepared for by 25 years of engineering experience, let alone four or five years of, ahem, school. If Linda was lucky in any way, it was that she was one of the first, and would have a head start on those who followed.

Ira Frank started at WED only a week after Linda, with many of the advantages and disadvantages. Ira did have a few years of engineering experience under his belt. In contrast to Linda's enthusiastic, direct approach to problem solving, Ira liked to really hash things out verbally before taking a course of action. He was known for starting his little speeches on why he was doing something a certain way with the word, "Essentially . . ." Ira was, essentially, messy. His office became a running self-joke with its papers piled upon papers upon books upon drawings upon whatever, trash mixing with vital documents in some sort of running Dadaist commentary on the world of engineering. There was also a live pine tree, a wall-sized map of Tokyo Disneyland and a plastic roast turkey.

Phil Beamish, an engineer who started several months after Ira and Linda, was another youngster. Phil had perhaps the perfect personality for a 510 employee, boasting the body of a body builder, the artistic sensibilities of a pianist, the mind of an engineer and an occasional stubbornness that would put the entire Mule Train through Nature's Wonderland to shame. In the 1048 building, Phil was two offices from Ira and the contrast was startling. Phil's office was often neat enough to make one wonder if he was out of town on business; his walls were decorated mainly with schematic diagrams and other such documentation. If nothing else can be said about Pixie Dust, call it the Great Equalizer – as different as they were, both Phil and Ira got their jobs done.

Chris Senchack's office lay between Ira's and Phil's, as was perhaps fitting. Chris' walls were neither as idiosyncratic as Ira's nor as stark as Phil's, and his personality was a fair mid-point between the two. Another engineer, Chris had traveled the world, in the army and out, and it seemed to have prepared him for many of the unusual aspects of 510. Still, he was no doubt the most high-strung of the engineers, and his nasal Texas twang could often be heard swearing "Oh nooooooo" at some engineering setback unseen by others in the building.

Glenn Birket, was 510's most laid-back engineer. He was the silent Cal of 510, his sturdy frame and dark, often brooding countenance hiding a relaxed, easy-going personality and high sense of professionalism. Stuck away along a back wall of the 1048 building, in an office shared with Linda, they were 510's junior engineers. The remarkable irony of this was their main office decoration – a huge poster of Peter Pan, the boy who never grew up.

In addition to these show control engineers, there were an equal number of audio and ride engineers.

Lee Frisius was the show section head. He was the man to whom all of the young show engineers reported. Barely older than his charges, Lee was expected to take this raw talent and mold it into a dynamic engineering force, a feat not unlike forming cut gems from diamonds-in-the-rough using your bare hands. Interestingly, at various times, Lee exhibited one or the other of the personality traits of many of his underlings – the enthusiasm of Linda, the solidness of Phil, the "high-strungness" of Chris, the introspective nature of Glenn and the slow approach of Ira. A computer could not have chosen a more fitting match.

Ralph Rosenthal was the original department 510 head. Ralph was one of those people whose good-natured hunch and Groucho-ish walk made him appear shorter and less imposing than he really was. He was not above putting his arm around an engineer with a smart remark and a caring, "Howzit going?" He was also not beneath coming down real hard on anyone whom he felt needed the pressure. Ralph was the number one guy at 510, and everyone knew it. Like many managers, he was equally respected and disliked by the 510 group.

Annette Tedrow was the executive secretary. Annette was one of those Midwest gems that Disney has a reputation for hiring, but are actually quite rare in the company. At times more of a public relation/employee relations director than anything else, Annette had the trying task of attempting to find out the answer to employee questions like why their Mickey Mouse buttons never arrived, how could they get some extra free tickets to Disneyland, how come there were no coffee cups in the break room and where in the hell were the managers when you had something to talk about? Annette handled the job with a certain cheery aplomb, and her constant candy and cookie handouts showed her dedication to her co-workers. Sweet as she was though, Annette had a business side that could snap a drill sergeant to attention, and when she called to "remind" you to get in your time sheet, engineers sometimes dropped the most important projects to get their butts in line.

John Brayman was a sort-of "coordinator." That's the kind of job where the actual job title changes two or three times a year, but what needs to be done stays pretty much the same. John was one of the few non-managers in 510 who hadn't heard a high school bell in the last 10 years. At times he seemed like the stern uncle of the group. Business was business to John, and the atmosphere of the growing department seemed to bewilder him at times. His background in the no-nonsense aerospace industry made it hard for John to accept the silliness, lack of planning and straight-on wrongness of much of 510's operation. He complained about many of the department's decisions, mostly to deaf ears, yet often had the smug satisfaction of watching his plans get implemented days, weeks or months later as someone reached the same decision independently. Because of this, he became regarded among some engineers as somewhat of a coot, and by others as a pretty right-on guy. His relationship with management was at times strained, but they did admire his ability to get the job done.

Ray Roberts was another coordinator. Ray had a lot in common with Ralph besides initials. Another wisecracker with a jaunty bounce in his step, Ray didn't have the stigma of being a manager that Ralph had, nor the aerospace background of John Brayman. This meant Ray usually got along much better with the younger engineers, who playfully teased him about his smoking, his age and his taste in clothes. Ray smart-mouthed with the best of them, exhibiting a salty demeanor developed through his love of the sea and sailing. (He even lived on a boat at one point.) Few 510 people had any reservations about helping Ray out with any favors.

Mark Gardner was the senior programmer. Mark was the 510 resident computer hacker, but was unusual in the respect that he had a couple of degrees to back up his wizard's cap, as opposed to many hackers, who, consumed by computers, barely graduate high school. Mark was unusually clean-cut, even for a Disney employee. He wore a short haircut, conservatively out-of-date clothes and was remarkably clean-shaven. Mark was the kind of guy who would seclude himself in a corner with a computer system (or two or three) and an armload of reference books, only to emerge hours or even days later with some wonderfully useful computer program. Software was The Answer to Mark, and he would write programs to do the simplest things, just because it could be done. Management and engineers alike scoffed at his often roundabout way of getting things done, but there was no denying his efficiency – he didn't seem to mind working 40 hours a week or 140. Locked in his office with a constant supply of soft drinks and junk food, Mark seemed ready to devote his entire life to the Disney ideal.

One of the signs of growth in a new society is the birth of children. In every corny movie that's ever been made about the Pilgrims, the West or even space, there's always a scene where the tough settlers gather about a crib to see the new baby, and we know that somehow, they're going to survive.

At WED, the society was not quite that primal, nor in a position to regenerate themselves through a new generation (they only had until October 1, 1982), but the engineers were given signs of hope by the infusion of co-op students. Co-ops were the kids among kids, babes among babes. They were college students brought in on work-study programs as a learning experience, and were considered the freshest transfusion in a department already full of new blood.

Actually, a few of the co-ops were older than some of the engineers, but for one reason or another, they were slow in getting their degrees. It was not so much a question of age as of attitude. For many of the co-ops, particularly those from Maine and the Midwest, the freakish pace of life in Los Angeles alone was a culture shock. It's a wonder they didn't turn and head for home after one day of being immersed in the insanity of pre-opening day department 510, which was akin to a whole coop of headless, yet still functioning, chickens.

In spite of an inevitable "gee whiz" attitude, most of the co-ops got down to business and began cranking out work as fast as the next chicken. They would never fear finals week again. Department 510 and all of WED were in the midst of one big, two-years-long finals week, and graduation was in October, 1982.

The Imagineers didn't need coffee for these finals, nor any other artificial stimulant. They were ripping along quite nicely on Pixie Dust, a drug with no side effects other than heavy addiction and a massive crash scheduled for opening day.

1048

Originally squeezed into the crowded loft of the MAPO building, it wasn't long before department 510 was forced to move into the "1048" building, isolated from the rest of the company by what grew in the minds of the engineers to be the longest city block in the history of city blocks, the quarter-mile stretch of gray, industrial Grand Central Avenue.

Between the chaotic dynamo of WED headquarters and the insecure brain trust of department 510 lay a dull, 10-minute walk along decrepit chain link fence and a motley bunch of bleak, Glendale-standard commercial/industrial complexes. It was a walk often made more distasteful by the tire-screeching, discourteous drivers of a nearby pay-TV firm. The engineers felt like abandoned children.

And rightly so. Isolated as they were from the core of the company corps, it was a difficult task to complete the simplest chores. Extracting a consensus on an engineering proposal might entail phone calls and visits to the main WED building, the Airway building, one of several multi-purpose buildings on Flower Street, the studio and for the truly tortured, the Tujunga building or Disneyland itself.

After a while, however, there was a growing acceptance and even a certain amount of pleasure derived from the 1048 building's location. After all, if an abandoned child is old enough, mom and dad can be a drag anyway, always looking over your shoulder, checking on what you're doing; so if they don't want you around, well hey – it's a lot more fun this way, anyway.

So the department settled into its new quarters. Everybody was scattered around the building, with management up front (of course), the technicians near the rear loading dock, engineers around the periphery. Wirelisters and word processors lined up along a long wall dividing the rear two-thirds of the building lengthwise, and drafters filled up the immense floor space in the center of the main room.

In short, it was a mess.

Engineers were strewn about the building with no regard to their projects; managers were divided from their teams by a maze of corridors so intimidating that visitors often got lost going from one area to the next, although the total length of hallway was less than 50 feet. In fact, new employees took days to get used to the scheme, and would often wind up in the bathroom when they really wanted a technician.

The bare, off-white uniformity of the building did nothing to help matters. There were no "landmarks" to aid in travels around the building. Something would have to be done before employees began leaving trails of breadcrumbs or tying string to their office doors alongside instructions for the inevitable search teams. Quickly the walls were covered with posters, strange newspaper clippings, cartoons, doctored photographs, Disneyana advertisements and even a fake turkey. And that was outside the offices.

Being normal was NOT normal in department 510 and new-hires learned quickly to unleash their personas if they didn't want to get lost in the woodwork. It wasn't that the WED engineers were any stranger than people in the outside world, it was just that the inherent dichotomy of engineering in an artistic company encouraged unrestrained non-conformance.

Inside, one could find almost anything stuck to the walls, from floppy disks to cheesecake (or beefcake) photos (and worse). The offices quickly became bizarre outcroppings of personalities, where people hung not dirty laundry, but their minds, souls, political and sexual persuasions, senses of humor – almost their entire beings – out for display. It was unusual for an engineering department, where

19

often the most exciting decoration in an office is a poster for a new microchip and an ASCII code table.

Adding to the carnival atmosphere was the constant ringing of telephones, which, unshielded by walls that failed to reach the ceiling, echoed across the engineering floor with constant intensity, surpassed at times only by the nasal tones of the operators calling for various lost souls over the paging system. At times, the resultant atmosphere resembled the floor of the New York stock exchange during a crash: engineers rushing to answer the phone ringing in their offices, engineers rushing to answer a phone that wasn't ringing in their offices, (a maddening illusion conjured up by the malicious properties of the wall construction), operators paging employees who were out to lunch, fired or completely bogus (as in, "Let's call the operator and have her page Kenny Rogers, heh heh.") and the ever-continual noises of computer printers, air conditioning, typewriters, phone conversations, guffawing, cussing at Things That Don't Work, electric erasers, radios, humming, pounding on desks (usually induced by Sony Walkmen), loud music from the audio lab and any number of minor and major sounds, some annoying, some pleasant, all indicating that things were being done.

Most of the time, the engineers just wanted silence, which meant that Real Work was being done. Most of the time, they didn't get anything approaching silence. If they were lucky, they were at least left alone. Everybody in the 1048 building simply learned to grin (or at least grimace) and bear it. After a while, only new-hires noticed the true insanity of the environment. And those few times when the building fell silent for whatever reason, there was a sort of cosmic eeriness that implied the immense unlikelihood of everything falling quiet at once, and people would pick up their phones to make sure the circuits weren't dead.

* * *

It was in this wonderfully relaxed, stressful atmosphere that nearly all of the electronic engineering for the most expensive theme park in the world took place.

Each engineer, technician, drafter, clerk and manager built a protective cocoon out of their personality, hunkered down in it, and prepared to do some kick-ass work for the duration of a project that everybody *knew*, from the outset, would never, ever finish on time.

And, despite their conflicting personalities, pathetic collective lack of experience (professionally or socially), and a near-complete dearth of any idea of what anyone was doing or was going to do, this strange slice of social strata would someday grow together, into a unit that would become a family as much for its closeness as its squabbles.

In this family was a core of siblings, completely indistinguishable from everyone else in the group, who possessed, planted somewhere in the fertile loam of their fates, a seed that would germinate and root them inextricably to one thing – building EPCOT.

Club 33

Behind the gentle tinkling of fine china and crystal, the soft patter of rain could be heard outside the elegant dining room. The room gave off the impression of graceful elegance without flamboyance. Freshly polished furniture and floors reflected the subdued candlelight, investing the room and its occupants with a warm and comfortable glow. A murmur of conversation and gentle laughter carried across the setting as patrons dined on imported cheeses, lobster tail, and crepes.

In marked contrast to this comfortable atmosphere, below the windows an occasional figure darted from one awning to the next across the rained drenched square. Some carried small children, others the paraphernalia of a family outing to Disneyland: Mickey Mouse balloons, guidebooks and packages laden with candies and curios. Yet despite of the weather, these visitors could enjoy that rare commodity: an uncrowded day in Disneyland. They were boarding boats in a sleepy bayou filled with electronic fireflies, to be entertained by a raucous band of carousing pirates, amidst cellophane fire, and a catchy soundtrack that repeats every 30 seconds.

Upstairs, Linda and her guests sat at a table near the window in the dining room of Disneyland's private club, the officially secret Club 33, watching the brightly colored tourists dart through the gray day, and drinking in all of the warmth the club offered. She had only worked for WED about six months, but as one of their few electronic engineers, she could enjoy the full benefits of a unique company's generosity through the club membership of the Vice

President of Engineering, John Zovich. His standing offer to make reservations for all engineers on his club membership was a unique benefit afforded the tiny engineering staff.

Other unique benefits included admission of oneself and guests to Disneyland, free rental of any of the company's films from the film library and, perhaps most importantly, the opportunity to work with the most unusual electronic control systems in the world.

American Adventure

In 1979 the electronic engineering department was comprised of barely two dozen persons, very few of whom had been with the company long enough to remember construction of Walt Disney World. And so hiring commenced. Little did 510 realize that this hiring was only the tip of the iceberg and that far more complex requirements would soon expand the job.

Soon the show section would find itself responsible for monitoring items throughout EPCOT, including air and hydraulic levels, electrical panels, and projectors. The ride section would be called upon to perform such complex tasks as guiding mammoth vehicles along a wire through a maze of doors. And the audio section would find itself responsible for speaker sequencing around one mile of parade route, and other complex signal processing tasks.

As these requirements became known, it seemed like a logical time to redesign the systems by which attractions were controlled, upgrading them from 1960's technology to new systems better suited to handing the complicated tasks demanded of them. So each section undertook the design of new systems that could be used throughout EPCOT. At the same time that these general-purpose tools were being designed, the attractions that required them were being defined, and so it was often necessary to begin the design of the attraction's controls before the tools were ready.

Glenn Birket describes those days:

I hired on with WED on November 5, 1979. I was assigned to American Adventure on that day. It sounded like an interesting pavilion. I knew it was one of the largest, and I knew that Jane, an ex-supervisor of mine from Operations in the Magic Kingdom was assigned as a coordinator to the pavilion. It would be fine working with her again.

There was very little information as to what the pavilion was all about. There were almost three years to complete the design and build it. That seemed like a lot of time then. I had no idea that the design wouldn't actually start for quite some time, and that there wouldn't be nearly enough time to do it. There wouldn't have been nearly enough time to do the design if I'd been able to start in November of 1979. I had no idea of the size of the task, no idea what I was up against. But I had a lot of optimism about it. It seemed a little odd to me that they would take a person right in the door, right out of school and assign them to what appeared to be a pretty big task without any experience to go on.

I didn't realize that I was going to have to design a system that had such great potential for doing harm to itself and other people. Nor did I realize there were almost no guidelines to go on. Even the control systems that existed at that point, which were few and far between, were very poorly documented.

When I expressed concern I was told 'There are experienced people around here who can give you some insight into this.' I found out later that all those experienced people where spread too thin and overworked. And not too long after that they started dropping by the wayside, one by one.

There was so little to do on American Adventure for the longest time, that it didn't concern me. I was put on a project to redesign the cards used to control the animated figures. I soon found out that what they really meant was 'Make these cards work with components that are on the market today but change them as little as possible.' They wanted complete *retrofitability* into their old systems. This often got me into awkward situations where minor redesign could vastly improve the cards. There was unbelievable resistance from management outside our department because of distrust. There had never been an electronic engineering department before, and they didn't trust our motives.

A lot of effort was expended to keep those cards from being changed in any way. So I dutifully went along trying to modify the cards as little as possible. There were some good people in the department later on like Mark and Marty to draw technical advice from. I learned a lot from those guys.

As American Adventure began to pick up speed I wasn't able to devote my full attention to the cards. There were many people who had their hand in it, and I don't think anyone ever had a clear and continuous impact. So the design came out haphazard at best. Most frustrating of all, it turned out that the cards wouldn't be retrofitable, for reasons beyond our control. Several redesigns were needed because of changes to other systems. Everyone right up the line to the vice-president now acknowledges that they made a mistake, and that they should have done a new design. But it was a very educational experience. It acquainted me with the old and the new, and the personalities and politics involved.

For a while I was assigned to the Seas pavilion, but I decided to hand it off to someone else because American Adventure was becoming one of the biggest and most difficult pavilions, and it was obvious that one would be enough. Some people took two or more of the smaller ones.

At first, American Adventure was very low priority. I received information on figures, and how many movements there would be per figure, the layout of the show, and so forth. I developed some ideas about how I would control the figures, the cabling, and the location of equipment. I couldn't get too particular at this point because the show was changing fairly often: how many figures, their functions, and the like. The special effects were very poorly defined in the beginning. Lighting was also very sketchy.

The show control system seemed very straightforward, although there was a lot of it. It was one of the biggest shows ever. I left lots of room available for lighting and special effects because there was so much definition left to be done in the show.

But the sketchiest area of all were the lifts and carriages that would position the figures on the stage. How were they going to be moved and controlled? I went to Wayne in the animation group. He said that the lifts didn't need to be treated any differently than a function in a figure. So I added those up and put them into the animation cabinets.

The movement of the carriages was being done by Ed Feuer, in the mechanical group. For the longest time it had been assumed that the carriages would be moved by Linear Induction Motors, using magnetism. But the details were very vague in the beginning, so I didn't do a lot of analyzing and commenting, just mostly watching. Perhaps if I had been more experienced I could have effected the design earlier in the project. But I wasn't confident enough.

As I began to calculate what was going to be required it became obvious that it was not going to be simple. I talked with a lot of people who had done work with LIM's before, and became convinced that it was not the appropriate approach.

Hence I embarked upon my first big adventure to change Ed's mind. With some help from Ralph, my department head, and Lee, my Section Head, I was successful in convincing management that LIM's were not the right solution, and that the carriage was better moved by a regular motor with a cable. So the mechanical people went to work on that system.

I learned a lot in that first adventure about dealing with the mechanical engineers, and Ed in particular. It was very difficult to get information out of him. He seemed to be very skeptical of electronics controls in general and me in particular. It was about this time that I found out that he had already tried to have me removed from the job. I can't blame him, given my inexperience, and his better perception of how big the job was.

It developed that Wayne was not going to do the design of the lifts after all. The design had been assigned to mechanical engineering rather than the animation group because the lifts turned out to be very big. The constraints placed upon the design of the lifts were:

They had to be portable, so they could be placed on the carriage.

They had to lift a load of several thousand pounds with an unknown center of gravity.

They had to be very quiet.

They had to lift the payload 14 feet in 10 seconds.

I didn't know much about hydraulics from my one fluids course, but I knew that was a very challenging assignment. What was even more challenging was keeping up with it from a control standpoint – not achieving it technically, but keeping up with the changes, the rhetoric and the poor communications.

Ed came up with a preliminary design. At this point he called me in and said that he would need a box with four switches: up, down, fast and slow. That seemed rather straightforward. All he wanted to do was to energize four solenoids.

This didn't seem much more complicated than the original approach. But before the box was even built it had evolved into a box with six switches.

Then the request came for automatic controls, requiring mechanical limit switches as sensors.

Another round of hydraulics changes led to a control system based upon integrated circuit logic. I threw this together on a prototyping board in a few evenings, and put it in a box with some switches.

This didn't prove to be sufficient, either. More complexity was added to the hydraulics. Many of the changes centered around the need to keep the three lifting cylinders of a lift synchronized so that one didn't go up faster than another, raising the lift crooked. So hydraulic complexity was added, entailing more electronic complexity in the control box, and finally a new control box. On the fifth or sixth modification of the third control box with three boards full of logic I began to question the validity of the design, and whether it was sensible to pursue it along those lines.

At this point in the prototype lift development I began to worry that we never going to get anywhere. We were eating up a lot of time on the development and I was anxious to get on with the design of the final system. We still didn't have any real information about the hydraulics. The changes seemed to be going on forever, with no end in sight. I had no idea how much, but I had a pretty good idea that I was compressing myself. We weren't submitting information regularly to the facilities engineering department for incorporation into the design of the building's electrical drawings. It was going to hurt, because they had already gotten through the groundbreaking of the building and we hadn't given them any information about conduit runs. The major runs had to be in at the same time the cement slab was poured, and they just weren't going to make it.

There we were, with the electronic engineering design not really begun and the building being put together.

A lot of other people were beginning to show the same concerns. At this point Bob M. was the Project Manager. Bob took a very weak position on the whole issue, and didn't seem to want to get involved. Jane was much more inclined to get involved. She seemed more sensitive to the problem.

As more and more hydraulic deadlines slipped it was finally brought to enough people's attention that a board of inquiry was established. This put Ed in a very difficult situation.

There are two sides to the story. Ed says that if he had been left alone the design would have been wrapped up. He still believes that the design that he was pursuing at that time was feasible. He may be right. There is no doubt that what he was put through slowed down his effort. He spent a lot of time justifying what he was doing. The end result was that other options were considered, and that after these meetings a major change in the design occurred.

But it was a long time after that meeting before Ed and I spoke to each other again, probably a month and a half.

After that meeting they came up with a new design, and a new commitment as to how many sensors and commands it would take – about six of each. Ed had a preliminary hydraulic schematic that showed that that was the most that could be required. Even the animation people agreed.

For the most part I believed what I was being told, although I suspected there might be some expansion, so I doubled the capability of the next box that I built, and made it computer controlled. A co-op student, Greg, wrote the software.

But even though I doubled the number of inputs and outputs we promptly filled all that up and had to jury-rig others. So we went through another development period that took much longer than expected, and compressed me into oblivion. Finally the point was reached at which we just had to guess.

As Ed began to see the flexibility of the new computer controlled system he began to appreciate and then take for granted these new capabilities.

Eventually Ed had to start ordering parts and building the thing, because the building was coming together in Florida. So he began giving me some limited information, but we determined that the development would have to continue right on into installation in Florida.

Learning from my earlier experience, I didn't hesitate to do what seemed to be a tremendous overkill at the time. I gave instructions to Brian Cox to design two portable lift controllers, for use in the Florida, since we knew we wouldn't have the real control system ready in time. They enabled us to reprogram from a terminal right next to the lift. We made two of them so that we could check out two lifts at a time. They were known as "Fred" and "Fredrica". We dreamed up a scheme for breakout boxes that standardized all the control and sense points on each lift, so that we could just plug and go.

In retrospect, that decision saved us.

By now it was late 1981. I made a pitch to Lee that the thing was getting bigger and bigger, and I needed some support. I wrote a memo detailing how much of my time I thought it was going to take to design American Adventure. It proved that I needed at least two more people to get the job done. His response was "Well, it seems unlikely. I don't understand how. But you've done a pretty good job of documenting it, so I'll give you one."

Along came Walt. There's no doubt that he was the right one to add at that point in the project. He had a background that could complement mine. He understood power and construction and the electrical drawings. And he works very hard when he's overloaded. I went over the show control system with him. He configured all of the animation cabinets to control figure functions, curtains, special effects and so on. Special effects and lighting were still very ill-defined, so we just designated empty cabinets for those. He had to procure special, short, reinforced, gasketted cabinets to take the punishment of riding on the lifts.

One day I found Walt doing the lighting. I hadn't wanted to get into the lighting at that point because it was so ill-defined, but he decided to get into it anyway. I had always intended to do everything myself, and it took me a long while to learn to delegate these things. So he started producing dimmer schedules and feeding information to the facilities people.

There's a lot of strange cabling in American Adventure, because of the flexible elevator cable that is used to get on and off the lifts and carriages. The facilities people were so overworked that they couldn't support us much, but fortunately Walt was familiar with the National Electric Code. But we never got information in time to get all the cables onto the drawings, so we had to do a lot of it in the field.

Bob M. was about to retire about this time, and because he was never a very forceful individual, Jane had been taking most of his responsibility, anyway. Jane was handicapped by her lack of technical background and familiarity with construction terminology. However she is very ambitious and dynamic, and capable of making decisions. If you needed visibility or a problem solved, she could get it for you. With Bob's retirement Jane was given the Project Manager position. She's a good manager.

The first thing she did was organize a tremendous push to get information to the facilities engineers. The push culminated in a meeting in her office, where I was pressed into, from memory, drawing over a hundred 25-pair cables on a rough sketch of the building floor plan. The drawing was based on a best guess from what little information I had. At this point the walls were up on the building, and the roof was going on, so we were very boxed in as to where cables could be run.

They were astonished at the amount of cable required. Their conceptions prior to that were based upon incomplete information about lifts, lighting and special effects, and amounted to less than 20% of the cable actually required.

I was stunned by how poorly the facilities people knew the building. They relied heavily on the architects. I had to recommend how to get the conduit from stage left to stage right, for example.

Another suggestion I made was for a computer floor. There was simply no other way to get cabling to the cabinets, once the concrete had been poured. They had all assumed that all the cabinets would be in the electronic equipment room. I had even assumed that until very late in the game. But it was just another example of grossly underestimating how complex the show was. The electronics equipment room couldn't begin to hold all the cabinets. In fact, audio equipment ended up filling the entire electronics equipment room. They couldn't run the cable overhead because it would have interfered with the projector's path. It's a good thing they didn't try, because as it turned out there would have been so much cable it would have completely obscured the view of the ceiling.

It probably worked out for the best, given how much of the design we ended up doing in the field. But it was certainly the most expensive and painful way to do it.

When Jane became project manager she asked for Nancy G. from WED coordination in Florida to be the coordinator for American Adventure. I had worked with Nancy, too, in operations years before. Melanie had been a planner for us all along, but at this point became much more involved as a team member. Shirley had originally been the planner, but later became the Project Business Administrator. The driving force behind the pavilion was always this group of four.

There's no doubt that my rapport with Jane and Nancy from years before changed the course of the project. Partly because of their lack of technical background, they have always almost blindly supported me, and that probably has a lot to do with why I was kept on the project.

I Built EPCOTAnd All I Got Was This Crummy T-Shirt

If there were a Dunn & Bradstreet rating for corporate company loyalty, no doubt WED would be at the top of the list. Not just because the atmosphere was electric, nor because of the excellent medical, dental and stock benefits, nor even because of the prestige of working for the Mouse.

No, WED and the entire Disney organization were at the top of the Fortune 500 of companies with happy workers because they bribed their employees. Starting on day one, WED employees were showered with a stuffstorm of calendars, posters, license plate holders, bumper stickers, buttons, animation cells, jackets, tee shirts, books, tickets to the parks, newsletters, ceramic figurines, telephones and a countless myriad of. . . things, all stamped with smiling mice, fairy tale castles and big silver geodesic domes.

Not all of it was free, but most of it couldn't be found or bought anywhere else in the world at any price. Walt only knows how many employees actually hired on at WED just so they could get a lot of neat Disney stuff.

As the deadline for EPCOT drew nearer, the company began throwing collectibles at the employees in an ever-quickening, Phoenician pace: more and more widgets, glory upon glory, all getting ready for the big Opening Day when, if the frenzy continued, all the employees would pile every Disney thing they owned in a heap on Sonora Street, touch a torch to the whole thing and jump on, in a flaming display of Mickey Mouse loyalty.

One set of items that became desirable was the set of buttons for each pavilion. Every month or so, WED distributed a brightly colored button containing the cryptic logo of one of the 10 Future World pavilions. Due to hoarding secretaries and pilfering employees, there were never enough to go around. So, on the days that a button was released, a line grew at the department secretary's desk with the fervor of a bunch of rabid gerbils.

If you couldn't get a button for a pavilion, you weren't anybody.

Employees wore the buttons, all of them, pinned into caps, vests and suspenders. Mysteriously, some people got the full sets before they were released. These lucky ducks were the object of much envy and resentment. Buttons became objects of greed and loathing. Great sums of money were offered for buttons by desperate employees who had missed out. Fear of missing out on a button day may have reduced sick time.

EPCOT countdown calendars were also a motivation for fear and loathing. One secretary hoarded calendars, giving them out only to her friends in the department and telling others, "There's only enough for salaried employees," or "Job shoppers don't get any." Later, someone happened by a garage sale at the secretary's home and saw piles of WED stuff on sale at exorbitant prices.

It got so bad that the entire set of calendars of one of the Florida field office secretaries was taken. She was crushed.

In Florida, the engineers had a problem getting their buttons and calendars at all. WED Florida wanted little to do with the administrative headaches of the Californians and WED California would just as soon have kept the buttons for themselves than send them across the country in the company mail. The big question in Florida was not whether EPCOT would open on time, it was "Hey, where are our buttons? They already have them in California."

WED also issued company tee shirts so employees could literally wear their hearts on their sleeves. There was such a demand for the tees, that in addition to official company releases, unofficial shirts were printed, such as the Imagineering tee shirt for Department 845 in Florida with Figment on it, the American

Adventure tee shirt, "I Love Department. 510," "We can do it" and "We did it" and "Official _____ Crew" (fill in the name of your favorite pavilion). And at the end, there was the most popular shirt of all, "Who built EPCOT? You're looking at him". Linda was mad that hers didn't say, "You're looking at her".

Open House

Naturally, a prime imperative as the company began sucking in employees like a giant overtime vacuum was to involve their families in the company as much as possible. Many employees became so wrapped up in their jobs that without corrective action, there would have been as many "Disney widows" and "Disney widowers" as there are football widows on Super Bowl Sunday. So WED took corrective action. Company picnics and outings sought to make everyone's family (or significant other or best friend for the singles) feel as much a part of the plan as the employee. And, of course, there were those free passes to the parks so you could take your family, etc. to see what you were working on.

But the coup de grace was the annual open house.

The open houses were the only time, ever, that one could bring his or her family or a close friend into the dream factory. The place where dreams were put together with nuts, bolts, magic and ingenuity opened its doors to the common folk, those pitiful souls fortunate enough to actually know someone who was permitted to enter the hallowed halls, yet unable for whatever reason to get in themselves.

Almost everyone was as excited as if they were preparing for the opening of the new projects. Employees began looking forward to work with new zeal. Offices were cleaned, walls were painted, bizarre decorations were taken down (or at least hidden), new posters and paintings were put up, carpets were shampooed, desks were polished, pencils were sharpened, burnt-out lamps were replaced, break areas were cleaned up and everybody rejoiced in the idea that they would soon share the Dream with their loved ones. Whistle while you work. Hi ho, hi ho.

And then, they handed out the tickets. That's right, not just anybody could walk in on open house day. It wasn't that the company wanted to limit the number of loved ones an employee could bring, but. . . There had to be reasonable limits. In their zeal, no doubt some employees would have brought greatly extended families, Aunt Babs, Uncle Alf, cousin Mark, second cousin Jean, Dog Rover, Boy George. . . You get the idea. There would have been a bigger crowd than Disneyland on the 4th of July. So there had to be a limit. Four tickets for singles. (Supposedly for your significant other, plus Mom and Dad.) Dependents for married-type folk. Period. No exceptions. Donald Duck couldn't have brought Daisy and Huey, Louie and Dewey (remember, they were nephews).

Of course, a black market in extra tickets soon arose. Singles were practically mobbed by their married friends. "C'mon Joe, I know you're not taking your folks. Just one ticket, pleeassse???" they'd beg. Sometimes Joe was easygoing and gave away his extras. Sometimes though, it could cost. "Okay," Joe'd say, "I'll trade it for that extra Tokyo groundbreaking pin you picked up when the secretary wasn't looking." And the ticket-needer would gnash his or her teeth and there would be a great moaning and rolling of eyes before an agreement could be made.

Invariably, everyone was able to work out something to his or her satisfaction by the day the doors opened. The Great Event was treated somewhat like the opening of the forbidden city of China to the people of the West. Outside the doors of the WED main building, reception tables were set up and WED's finest would line up to receive tickets and greet the unwashed masses. Mickey and Minnie were there. Carl Bongiorno, president of WED, and John Zovich, vice president of engineering, were there, along with assorted other high-level executives. And they would line up and shake hands with the employees and their families and act like they actually *knew* each and every employee, much to everyone's delight. (A brilliant illusion conjured up by a quick glance at the name tags.)

Everyone who entered was given a pass to stick on their blouse or shirt, which said, "WED Open House – Honorary Imagineer." The families and employees would beam with pride, because they were now more than intruders, more than snoopers in the Dream Factory. They were now members of the club. Everybody inside WED on open house day became one of the privileged few.

What a privilege it was! Guests to the open house were treated to sights that no mere visitor to the parks would ever see: the building of animatronics figures, sound system demonstrations that shook the walls, animated scenes being programmed, sets being designed. It was a Bacchanalian Disneyfest of the latest and greatest in entertainment technology for the masses.

The special effects department had working volcanoes spewing lava; the figure programming department had the slave-selling scene from Pirates of the Caribbean, complete with the scurvy dogs yelling, "We wants da redhead!." There were tapes of Country Bear Jamboree in Japanese, an audio animatronic Ben Franklin climbing a staircase, miniature model sets elevated to shoulder level so you could stick you head through a slot and walk through, viewing the ride from a realistic perspective. There were holograms, digital recordings, video tapes, computers with touch-sensitive display screens, plastic and cardboard models, sculptures, giant molds of African animals, costume displays, lifelike small animals, full-size sets, and above all, there were the employee offices, where you could see your loved one's name prominently displayed on an imitation engraved simulated wood plaque, showing that he or she was solidly entrenched in the middle of it all, with proximity to an awe- inspiring array of sheer genius of every type imaginable. "See, this is where *I* work! Right next to the dinosaur designers."

Of course, department 510 was there too, stuck down in the magnificently clean, prefabricated office building, a figurative 94 miles from the center of everything. The building was nearly deserted the entire day. Employees led their families through with a sort of proud embarrassment. "Gee, ma, I know it's a block away, but we go to the WED building for lunch." The families of engineering department personnel were treated to such intensely fascinating displays as the drafting department's drawing tables, the wirelister's computer terminals, the drafting/design department's exciting display of a $500,000 machine that could actually draw circles (when it wasn't broken) and a Houston WEDway-related display of a small, train-like vehicle that would actually go all the way around an oval track if you flipped a switch. The whole thing was so thoroughly exciting that anyone who had nothing to do with engineering stayed away.

The highlight of the engineering department's open house display was, brace yourself, a talking bird from the Enchanted Tiki Room.

That's all.

The young and brilliant minds of the management and employees of Department 510 suffered from a case of creative retardation so severe, the most exciting display they could come up with, year after year, was a talking bird. One wirelister was so frustrated, he wrote a program on the wirelisting computer that twinkled stars on the video screen as an EPCOT logo floating across the screen grew in size as if it were being approached by a star cruiser. Anything different to look at. Of course, by mid-morning, the computer had crashed, leaving a bunch of garbage on the screen as if Klingons had snuck into the 1048 building when no one was looking and blown up the EPCOT logo.

Even the accounting department had a more exciting display than department 510.

Still, no one was really disappointed. The spectacle of the rest of open house made up for any disappointment from individual departments. One year, the company set up a giant circus tent, then filled it with people in foreign costumes serving international foods in honor of EPCOT's World Showcase. Visitors thought the open house was terrific on account of that one attraction alone. It must have cost WED tens of thousands of dollars.

Project Stages

Everybody knew that a lot of overtime was going to be involved in the completion of EPCOT. Nobody knew that EPCOT would essentially become another word for one's waking hours. At least, if they did, they kept their mouths shut – wisely.

By January 1982, the 510 crew was put on a mandatory 50-hour work week. Actually, most of the engineers were already working at least that much. It was the support staff, the clerks and secretaries and blueprint machine operators and wirelister, whom the directive most affected. The engineers had grumbled about the lack of support when they were working overtime, their inability to get that crucial schematic at 6:00 p.m., so BAM! everyone was put on 7-to-6 time, with an hour for lunch.

The Great Scimitar of Opening Day was beginning its first wide swing through the Pixie Dust sky. Some people groused, some swore they would refuse, but only one or two people quit. But fifty hours was a drop in the bucket for most of those already in Florida.

There were a more than a few complaints here and there, but slogans such as "We can do it" and "The 21st Century begins October 1, 1982," were the order of the day. As the overwhelming overwhelmability of the job became apparent, a sign went up on some of the bulletin boards in the department. It said:

STAGES OF A PROJECT:
1. Assignment of responsibilities
2. through 6. Whatever
7. Shooting of the responsible parties

Everyone was joking that it would be the wirelist group that would be shot; that every mistake in every electronic cabinet, whether it was from bad design or poor quality control, would be a thorn in the crown the wirelisters would wear on opening day. They were going to accept the blame for everything that went wrong at EPCOT.

Of course, this was mostly joking, but there was enough truth and historical precedent in it that the wirelisters began taking their jobs very seriously. Under the keen eyes and stern management of John Brayman, they became the most reliable group in the department. Always on time and nearly perfect in every job. It would be tough to hang a typo on them, let alone the failure of a project.

Soon, signs started popping up all over the department, not dangerous signs of discontent, but harmless, healthy expressions of swimming in a whirlpool that was a little scary, but a fun ride nonetheless.

There was one sign that said, "In the course of every project, there comes a time when it becomes necessary to shoot the engineers and start production." One of the wirelisters (perhaps Phronie), altered it to say, "...to shoot the engineers and start wirelisting." Chris Senchack hung it up in his office.

WED put out some signs of its own, in a slightly misguided but well-intentioned effort to lift morale. The signs were part of a campaign that declared, "WE CAN DO IT!" It was obvious that whoever came up with the idea had little actual contact with the day-to-day chores and tribulations of the "crew." The signs were no doubt designed by some personnel committee that had enough of their own doubts about opening day to decide that we needed psychological encouragement instead of more pay or fewer hours.

Of course, the employees sensed the Madison Avenue phoniness of the campaign. They knew they could do it, they just didn't know exactly how. The "We Can Do It" stickers that were handed out were chopped up and rearranged, sort of like an anagram. People made their own sayings, such as, "WED did it to me" "Can It, We Do" and, of course, "Can We Do It?"

Another sign that appeared, with a more realistic tone, was one showing an engineer (or perhaps a manager), standing on top of a box of electronic components, cramming them into the box. The engineer is explaining to a curious onlooker, "It's got to fit, there isn't time to redesign it."

There did, however, seem to be time to redesign the 1048 building that housed department 510. As the department grew, the building changed from an empty warehouse, to a warehouse with a bunch of desks and drafting tables loosely scattered throughout, to a densely packed maze of offices and cubbyholes, complete with areas open to authorized personnel only. Many employees were shocked when a long-overdue security guard was hired to watch the exits, as if they suddenly realized valuable and secret things were taking place. The growth of the department was so constant that in spite of its magnitude, one paid little attention to it and it was only when slapped in the face by the sudden appearance of five new offices in a once open floor space, or being asked to show your ID tag at the door, or being told the Computer Assisted Drafting area was off-limits that you actually could sit back and gasp in amazement at how things had really changed in the last couple of months.

It is no less than amazing that the 510 engineers were able to take in stride the geographic shock (mental if not physical) of being moved from a cramped hallway above the electric shop, to an empty, nondescript warehouse, to a sophisticated network of offices, to another empty, nondescript warehouse 3,000 miles away, to a trailer in a field four miles from the warehouse, to a field service office beneath EPCOT itself to, finally, a room filled with gleaming, humming metal rods across from a smelly garbage compacter somewhere in the bowels of CommuniCore.

All in less than two-and-a-half years.

But we get ahead of our story here.

A Dose of Reality

In the midst of the confusion, it became apparent that some attractions were going to go down to the wire before opening, and a few would not make it by opening day. As WED began to realize the scope of the task, a number of pavilions scheduled for opening day were postponed. One such pavilion was Horizons, sponsored by General Electric, which was delayed until October 1st, 1983. Also Seas and Life and Health, for which sponsors had not been found.

Part of the reason for the delays, oddly enough, was the division of labor in WED. Departments throughout the company were split between Tokyo Disneyland, Fantasyland Rehab, the Matterhorn rehab and EPCOT itself. Although it baffled some employees that WED was not committing all its heart, brain and soul to one project at a time, the company clearly had the right idea in taking advantage of the electricity-filled atmosphere to charge all its projects with a deadline-meeting life force.

Meanwhile, other companies and countries were clamoring to sponsor pavilions, but were told that they will not open by opening day. Morocco was scheduled to open by October 1st, 1984. Several pavilions originally intended to be full-scale attractions were scaled back, including Morocco and Denmark, which would begin life as restrooms. As a hold-over from their pavilion days, even the restrooms would have computers to control the parade route. Jokes were made about making rides out of the urinals. Ironically, it turns out that the park function controller in EPCOT Central will monitor the flushing of privies throughout the park.

In a strange reversal of what was happening in some of the other pavilions, Mexico, which had been scheduled to open December 1, was rescheduled for October 1 at the last moment when management decided they needed the extra crowd-handling capacity. This was just one more Excedrin headache for the engineering staff. It was decided that to relieve some of the burden of this unpleasant surprise, about half of the ride would be eliminated.

The people of department 510, accustomed as they are to half-empty warehouses, will get to share one with the public on opening day.

Soon, fervent attention was paid to attractions that had been so glaringly ignored that their state of ill definition threatened their very construction, with cement being poured where conduit should have been. The EPCOT Central Show was not designed until three long nights in April, when, in a blitzkrieg of activity Phil, Linda, Chris, and the wirelist group sat down and designed the entire show control system.

One of the first visitors to the site was John "Sully" Sullivan, who spent several months measuring cable, often with the help of his assistants Jenny and Derek. Guessing the length of cables through conduit that often didn't exist yet, or traversed a course through an inaccessible or often inscrutable maze, proved a real challenge. And if a cable was even one foot too short, hundreds of feet had to be pulled out and a new one laid. Engineer John Noonan was another one of the first people that 510 sent "to the field." He spent much of his time covering projects before the engineer in charge was sent down. Before opening day, John flew off to Tokyo Disneyland for that installation.

The departure of one engineer, less than a year before opening, rocked 510. Particularly affected was Linda, who suddenly went from project responsibility on two pavilions to 10 pavilions, many of them containing theaters. And most of the design work on those theaters had not yet been done. For weeks she was pestered for late information from a half dozen Project Managers whom she had never even heard of. Her responsibilities included France, Canada, China, UK, Germany, Denmark, Japan, Italy, and four cabinets from CommuniCore, in addition to Canada and World of Motion.

Many of the systems themselves had still not been designed; the intercom cans and the show start and stop buttons had not been done and the monitor system was just in a conceptual stage. They had nothing but circuit boards until Brian whipped together the first monitor cabinet.

Every few months a film detailing the progress on the EPCOT site was shown at WED. Each film built to the same inspiring climax, wherein an aerial fly-by was capped with a song, "We're Getting Ready," written especially for the project. At the end of the film, the camera sailed out over Spaceship Earth. There, at the very top, was a construction worker, waving. Spread out behind him, still invisible to all but the most enlightened, hung the Great Scimitar.

Welcome To MyMechanical Nightmare

By January of 1982 no work had really been done on the stage control, lighting, special effects controls or monitoring systems for the American Adventure. One day, word came down through the ranks that Carl Bongiorno, president of WED and Dick Nunis, head of Walt Disney World, had stated that EPCOT would not open unless American Adventure and Spaceship Earth were ready. Since everyone *knew* that EPCOT would open no matter what, this translated in the responsible engineer's minds as, "You don't want to know what will happen to you if this attraction doesn't open on time."

The engineering of American Adventure began late. Far too much time was spent building prototype control hardware for the ever-changing lift design under test in a parking lot in Glendale. Glenn's appeals for support were finally heard and two consultants, Bob and Steve, were hired in January 1982. Only the conceptual design had been done on the control system for the complex stage equipment required in the American Adventure pit. Dozens of cabinets were required. With Opening Day less than 9 months away Glenn requested and was given an expediter to circumvent the normally sluggish production process for cabinets and parts procurement. He was also assigned a designers, engineers, engineering aides, and technicians. This team approached the engineering of American Adventure in a completely different way than the rest of the engineering organization. This was possible due to the limited time available, greater human resources and the carte blanche treatment given to American Adventure by management.

The first thing Glenn made clear was that this team was going to do absolutely everything on its own, depending on no one. Production control would be bypassed. Custom systems would be designed to handle the control of the stage, eliminating any dependence upon other electronic design groups. The team would even have its own expediter.

This decision was the result of the poor response that all of engineering had been getting from the much dreaded Production Control organization, which reliably took months to procure parts for and schedule the assembly of cabinets released by engineering. There came a time when those months were no longer available.

This was really just an amplification of several techniques developed by the engineers before the crunch, to redefine the way things got done at WED and MAPO. During the '70s WED and MAPO had been small. Barely 200 people were left after the layoffs following Walt Disney World's opening. Department 510 didn't even exist. The design work was done by a very few people, with offices upstairs above the MAPO electric shop. When a piece of equipment was to be built it was sketched and taken downstairs to the technicians. But as WED geared up for EPCOT, suddenly there were forms, paperwork, scheduling, and even whole departments to manage the production process. The Production Control organization was created. Suddenly it began to take three to four months to get something done that could have been done in a week before. 510 was moved away from the MAPO electric shop into a building of its own. A new inventory control system called MIMS just created more paperwork rather than aiding in the procurement and construction of equipment.

To circumvent these bottlenecks, the engineers began informally circulating documents to those who needed them prior to the actual arrival of documentation from Production Control. In many cases this resulted in the work actually being completed before the work order was ready. It became common practice for unreleased prints to be sent to Florida so that those in the field could work in the pavilions preparing conduit runs and measuring cable and sizing circuit breaker panels. By the time the released prints made their way through the system, the conduit the specified was under eight inches of cement.

So Glenn's team really just carried this process to its logical conclusion. They designed their own ride control system; built their own cabinets; programmed their own monitor cabinet; debugged their own animation equipment; tested their own Show Control Unit in EPCOT Central; and handled virtually every other aspect of the electronic engineering themselves. They had their own grease monkey, Derek, their own electrical power specialist, Walt, their own ride computer programmer, Bob, Their own technician, Frank, their own expediter, Sonya, their own designers, Chuck and Martin, their own drafter, Betty, and their own hardware engineer, Steve.

The first action of the team was to divide the stage control system design into hardware and software design tasks. Bob was assigned the software tasks while Steve handled the hardware. Safety of the system was a critical issue, to prevent it from tearing itself apart and to avoid injuring anyone. It became essential to release all designs by March.

The American Adventure pit is an area below the stage in which a gigantic steel carriage, 60 feet long, 30 feet wide, and 14 feet high rolls from underneath the audience to position 10 hydraulic lifts in the proper spots so that they can rise behind the front lip of the stage, in front of the rear projection screen that spans the stage. At the rear of the building, behind the pit is a projection room, elevated three stories, from which a 70 mm film is projected onto the screen behind the figures. The show traces the history of America from the arrival of the Pilgrims to man's landing on the moon. Throughout the show, stages rise in front of the screen to allow audio-animatronic figures to act out important episodes in the history of America, while behind them scenery is projected.

The design of the show presents many potential problems, both aesthetic and logistical. For example, normal motion picture film jitters up and down constantly. In a movie theater, the eye, having no fixed point of reference, tracks it, so that we are unaware of this motion. However, when projected behind a fixed object such as a figure this motion becomes very noticeable. Elaborate pin registration devices must be installed to prevent the film from moving so that it simulates a fixed background.

Safety concerns in American Adventure resulted from the way the figures were positioned in front of the screen. The figures are extremely heavy, laden with hydraulic and pneumatic hoses, electrical wiring, solenoids, and a rigid metal frame. They are installed on large sets, ranging from a plaster rock to a building or a submarine. The entire assembly, weighing as much as 60,000 pounds, is raised 14 feet in 10 seconds under hydraulic control by one of four computers. When the pistons and feed valves are energized the set rises into position in front of the rear projection screen.

However there are far more sets than can possibly fit into the space between the proscenium at the front of the stage, and the rear projection screen, so 10 of the sets are mounted on a steel carriage, 14 feet high, 30 feet wide and 60 feet long. This carriage, resembling the framework of a boxcar, rolls in a pit. From underneath the audience it proceeds to the back of the building far behind the rear projection screen. It stops at six different positions during the show to enable lifts of varying sizes to be raised in the small gap between the back of the stage and the rear projection screen. Each lift weighs from 30,000 to 60,000 pounds, and the entire carriage of 10 lifts weighs on the order of half a million pounds. It must roll in absolute silence and without vibration during even the most quiet moments of the show.

Because of the weight of the lifts, the hydraulics must be capable of exerting extremely large amounts of force. However this means that if a lift is ever commanded to go up accidentally when it is underneath the concrete floor beneath the audience or below the rear projection screen, it will do irreparable damage to the figures, scenery, and whatever is above it. As a result, Glenn, Bob and Steve designed an elaborate system of safeguards and interlocks into the stage control system.

To further complicate matters, a second carriage rolls crossways to the first, simulating a raft floating down a river across the stage. The raft is mounted to the front of this smaller carriage on a hinge, and is raised into position when needed. The small carriage can roll so far forward that the raft is over the large carriage, so it must be up during this movement to avoid a collision. An additional lift, mounted on the small carriage, is raised while the small carriage is about half way through its travel. This lift must not be allowed to rise while the small carriage is under the curve of the rear projection screen. Nor can the small carriage be allowed to move the raft over the large carriage when figures have been raised from it. Or vice versa. Finally, there are various set pieces that are extended above the lift, such as the roofs of some buildings. These too must be in the fully down position or the carriage will not clear the structures above it. In all, it is a control nightmare.

The mechanical design was changing from week to week. This had a gross impact on an already partially completed electronic control system. It must have been redesigned a dozen times. Worst of all, the American Adventure prototype lift controller was still bending metal out in the parking lot of the mechanical engineering building.

Swampland

The first person from 510 to actually visit the site and come back was John Canton. When John returned, there was a section meeting. The tension was really high. The engineers sat around the conference table. Lee sat back and said, "Well, John, tell us what it's like down there."

And so John began.

He recounted tales of the mud, the construction workers, the unending work hours. And he kept saying, "They'll never finish it on time. They'll never finish it on time. It's crazy down there." Everybody came out of that meeting with a sense of gloom, but underlying it was the attitude, "Hell, if anybody can finish it, we can".

***

Spring brought talk about the Pixie Dust exodus – the move to Florida, the great relocation that was sure to come – and many engineers were saying "I'll work any hours they ask me to, but I won't go to Florida."

It wasn't really surprising. Many marriages were already straining as one spouse woke up an hour earlier and came home an hour later. The 3,000-mile separation was not something anyone relished and at the time no one really knew how the company would handle it. Would the entire family be able to go? Would they want to? What if both husband and wife worked? Would one have to consider giving up a job to accompany the other to Florida?

It was a question swept under the carpet for some time. Most of the 510 engineers were single men, and since the company considered non-marital relationships as fairly valueless, they were sent to Florida on the understanding that they could do without their girlfriends as long as the company deemed necessary. This turned out to be a cold but fairly accurate analysis of the situation by WED. No significant problems arose in the early days of relocation. As it turned out, anyone going to Florida for less than six weeks was considered to be on a "business trip." These people got $35/day per diem, a car, a place to stay and that's about it.

If you went for more than six weeks, you were on "temporary permanent relocation." You got all the benefits of a business trip, but the company didn't pay for your gas. (Would they fly your spouse out?) Oh, and you got a cheesy $22/day car.

Those fortunate or unfortunate enough (it all depended on your perspective), to be sent out for 6 months or more could have their families and furniture sent out with them, and were put up in semi-permanent lodging. This was "permanent permanent relocation," although the understanding was that it was really temporary and would end when EPCOT opened. These people didn't get any per diem after 30 days.

The company avoided the higher levels of relocation by sending people out on consecutive business trips, one after the other, with trips home for a week or so in between. Or they would temporarily relocate employees, bring them home for a month, then send them back on several consecutive business trips. Whether the company saved any money or not is moot, but they saved a lot of morale because the overwhelming first impression of most engineers at the thought of "permanent permanent" relocation was sheer terror.

***

A subtle change began to take place as more and more engineers made the pilgrimage to EPCOT. Each had so far successfully avoided any hint of panic, and although they were all very busy, they now began to make the long journey toward frenetic. None of us really had any idea what the site would be like, for the simple reason that words could not describe it. The solid, unending din of construction machinery, earth movers, buses of union laborers, trucks of carpenters, cement mixers and, more than anything else, the somehow tangible, tingling, torrent of raw energy produced by thousands of people, each operating at maximum output.

The Great Relocation began, in a slow, calculated way to allow the Pixie Dust to sink in. The first engineers to go to Florida from California were handpicked by management. The early moves were tempered by short trips back to California, during which each newly-transplanted engineer spoke with solemnity about the great tasks ahead, describing the great amount of work to be done and the great endurance it would take to complete it at all on time.

Funny thing–it worked. One by one, almost the entire engineering department was shipped to Florida, with little public dissent. Those not sent to EPCOT were sent to Japan for the important-but-hardly-as-visible Tokyo Disneyland project, or kept home to work on the "oh-yeah-how-is-that-coming-along" Fantasyland rehab at Disneyland.

***

"During the time that I spent in Florida," says Linda, "because the company was giving us first class tickets every six weeks, I thought of the distance between Los Angeles and Florida as no big deal - just five hours. Especially during the first six months, when I was traveling back and forth quite a bit. I went down there in late June and I was there for three months right before opening. About a week before opening I made a quick trip back into L.A. because Lee was having his going away lunch and I wanted to be there to surprise him. That was a thirty-six hour trip. I took the 4:50 p.m.

Delta non-stop out and the Red Eye back. A few weeks later my grandmother became ill, so I went back to see her on the grand opening weekend. I also went back at Thanksgiving, and then Christmas. During the early part of '83 I must have made seven or eight round trips. I had it all nailed: where I liked to sit in the airplane, what I was going to eat, what I was going to drink. For a long while you couldn't get on any Delta non-stop without running into a half dozen people you knew. There would be Wathel Rogers, or Rick Rothschild, or any number of engineers."

Many were the minor mishaps of building EPCOT, almost overlooked, or at least accepted with tolerance amidst the avalanche of responsibility. David's bicycle, a projector for Spaceship Earth, and Chuck's microwave oven were all shipped together on one of the thousands of trucks from California that made the long journey. After waiting several weeks it still hadn't arrived. David went to the warehouse asking, "Where's my bike? I want my bike." It turned out that the entire truck had been picked up by a tornado somewhere in Texas. With a $200,000 projector lost they couldn't have cared less about his bike.

The Company shipped hundreds of loads of boxes back and forth as a service to relocated workers. Bob Bombach even shipped the antique wheelchair that he used as an armchair in his living room. He had written a book about victrolas called "Look For the Dog," and wanted to get a supply of the books to Florida, so he gave a carton of them to anybody that was being relocated.

***

As each engineer from 510 made their first pilgrimage to the site, the same rituals were performed again and again. The first big step was buying your first pair of steel-tipped construction boots. David remembers that the first thing he did before walking onto the Site was to stomp through the biggest mud puddle he could walk through without drowning, so that he wouldn't look like "The new guy on the site".

Footwear became an important issue. Some engineers tried to rough it with tennis shoes, but, especially in the early days, that could prove a serious mistake. Those who had always regarded tennis shoes as real shoes, suddenly felt as if they were walking barefoot. In American Adventure there was so much hydraulic oil that any soles other than neoprene were dissolved, creating the distinct impression of walking on ice. Yet through it all, Brian religiously wore his Keds, crawling over rocks and boards with nails in them and big chunks of cement with pieces of cable sticking out. He'd climb merrily over a mountain of debris where mortal engineers would invariably twist their hiking boot-encased ankles.

Every 510 transplant had a different way of forging a working relationship with the construction workers. Jenny earned her stripes by taking them chocolate chip cookies.

***

Steve describes his arrival in Florida:

It was hard to believe, I realized as I got off the plane in Orlando. Less than 10 days before, I had been working under amazing pressure on a project that was far enough away, that I really had trouble understanding why there was pressure at all. And now, quite suddenly it seemed, I was here in Orlando, Florida, to work on a billion-dollar fantasy for which I had almost no qualifications.

What kind of insane misdirective had landed me in Walt Disney World for an undetermined amount of time, with a company car, a place to stay, all the free recreation I could endure, and per diem to boot? And I didn't even know what I would be doing or where I would be working.

Neither did any one else, it turned out.

I remember trying to put all of my earthly possessions into storage, separating little pieces of memorabilia and the bare essentials for the journey, in a hopeless attempt to preserve some fragment of home life. Linda had taken her margarita glass and chip basket stolen from Rusty's Hacienda, the favorite Friday lunch haunt of the 510 women.

One of those strange trademarks of the Disney organization, was the policy that employees flew first class. We all regarded it as a silly, unnecessary expense, but found, after several cross-country trips, that it was a policy one could quickly grow accustomed to. That first time I flew with Brian, who had been to EPCOT before.

The plane had arrived in Florida about five o'clock in the evening. I remember being impressed by how modern and attractive the airport was. I had three or four suitcases, one of them big enough to stuff a body into, plus a camera bag and a few other things. There weren't any porters and there weren't any baggage carts, so I had to struggle with it across the terminal, gradually stacking it up in front of the automatic door. The moment I stepped through the door a blast of humidity hit me. I thought, "Oh my God." I just couldn't believe it. It was raining. Warm rain. I had never felt warm rain before. It was like being in a shower. There were lakes at the airport, with egrets, heron and fish.

I picked up my rental car 10 feet outside the door of the airport and followed Brian onto the Bee Line Expressway, in awe at the verdant countryside: rolling swampy meadows covered with trees. Within a year they would be covered with industrial parks, but in 1982 it was virgin forest as far as I could see.

Nearly everyone's first visit began the same way – getting lost. The instructions that they gave us to get there weren't very good at that point, and finding the back gate to Walt Disney World on a little country road in the middle of the night could be a challenge. We had all been warned to stay away from "Johnny's Corner," where all the red-necks went at the end of the workday, and so, of course, we all ended up there after our first wrong turn.

I finally ended up at the Fort Wilderness resort. As I checked in for a two-week stay, little did I realize that I was registering for nearly the next two years of my life. There was an armadillo walking along the road as I drove to my trailer. That gave me an idea of what living in Florida was going to be like. I wasn't really expecting the mobile homes to be as nice as they were, or so separated by forest. My trailer was in Bobcat Bend.

Glenn had left a radio for Brian at the reception outpost, so after we were settled, Brian called him on the radio. Glenn was at American Adventure. We drove out to the site in Brian's car by the circuitous route that formed the only access at the time. My first view of the site was the white top of Spaceship Earth, looming above the forest. It was 180 feet tall, but there was no way to get any sense of scale. It was surreal.

Coming out of the forest, a mile of chain link fence stretched into the distance. I had the impression I was in a military compound. At the guard gate was a stern-faced security officer. We were nervous about trying to talk our way past him because we had no site ID's, but Glenn had contacted him and told him to expect us, so he let us through the gate. I was left with the impression of ultra-tight security, how secret the project was, how the media was being kept out by Disney's own army.

As we drove around the perimeter road of the site, all I could see were the black, gloomy hulks of buildings. There was a lot of debris, mounds of dirt, hunks of cement, scrapped building materials. We pulled up to the back of American Adventure. It was really dark, except for a couple of spotlights shining here and there on buildings. There was the sound of generators – far away? perhaps not – in the hot, humid night air. Frogs and crickets were closer.

The rear wall of the building loomed above us. There was a guard at the back door.

Stepping inside, I was astounded by how cavernous the building was. There was no more light inside than in the night sky. I could see all the way up through the pit, through the opening for the curtain, two stories above me, and to the rear of the theater, four or five stories above, and hundreds of feet away. Directly above me was seven stories of space, filled with black steel mesh and other nearly indiscernible objects. The main carriage, like several abandoned boxcars, had been assembled to the point of framework, with most of the hydraulics and (I knew) all of the controls missing. "My God," I thought, "this is supposed to open in six months?"

Glenn was the only person inside. It was at least eleven o'clock at night by this time, and he was sitting in front of a computer terminal – just a blue glow in the darkness – tinkering around with a program to move one of the lifts.

Glenn took us on a tour of the building. The stairways were not in place, so we wound through a bizarre route to get from room to room. The floor plan was so odd that at times we had to exit by one door and enter another. We took ladders made of two-by-fours to get between the various floors, at times crawling under scaffolding in pitch darkness.

Glenn led us out onto the roof by flashlight. The top of the building hadn't been completed. Standing at the edge, it was absolutely quiet except for the sound of distant generators. The only sight, as far as the eye could see, was EPCOT Center. I stood for a long time, that night, thinking about the months ahead.

* * *

The next morning was Steve's first daytime visit to the site. Driving up, he could see the black underlying framework of Spaceship Earth, only partially covered with white triangular skin. As he entered the guard gate, the first thing that struck him was the energy level. Getting out of the car at the PICO (Project Installation and Coordination Office) building, he could hear thousands of horsepower of machinery humming, hammering and hacking. There seemed to be thousands of people scurrying about carrying this, looking for that, injecting their very life's essence into this project. It was like the electric feeling in the air at a rock concert just before the main act comes on.

There was just a little water at the bottom of the lagoon. The islands seemed much larger. The sea wall was in, but there was no pavement at all, all the way around the World Showcase, a veritable mud-pit swarming with bulldozers, caterpillars, construction workers, and swamp bugs. Spaceship Earth had about two-thirds of the covering installed so that it looked like a gigantic white "happy face" with a black smile at the bottom.

Steve describes the scale of EPCOT this way: "The first time I ever got any real sense of scale on the site was after they paved around part of World Showcase in the early summer. It was the first time that Linda and I were at the site at the same time. We had each been sent down on several trips, but finally at the end of June we both arrived to stay. We went out and we walked hand-in-hand from American Adventure past France, and U.K., which had just been poured. When we got over towards Canada we were afraid that the cement was still wet, so we walked with extreme care. It took a long time to walk from American Adventure to Canada because there were many unpaved areas and obstacles in the way. I finally began to realize that we'd been walking for twenty minutes to get to someplace 'nearby' that I'd been looking at across the lagoon for months."

* * *

Per diem. That is the "business expense" money WED employees received while staying in Florida. $35 a day for the first month, and $22 a day thereafter. Hundreds of dollars a month of non-taxable income. Nearly as much as some were taking home. More than enough to live on in those days, considering that Disney also provided a free furnished mobile home in Fort Wilderness, its $95-a-night "campground" at Walt Disney World. Plus a car and gas. Certainly enough benefits to erase any perception that one's hours were sneaking up toward three digits a week, or that some were already serving more time than prisoners. Enough benefits, in fact, to make people feel downright guilty.

Andrew "complained" once, "This is sick, why do they give us this stuff?" It took Andrew a while to adapt to the large new American car and the full maid service every day. But few ever refused any of the benefits. Brian once refused to let the maid into his trailer. The maid badgered him to be allowed in, but he was mad because she kept turning his air conditioner on. He turned it off for about a week, until things started to grow in his carpet. He finally realized that you must have an air conditioner when the humidity is greater than 90% most of the time. After that, leaving a "Do Not Disturb" sign on his door did no good once he left his trailer; the maid cleaned anyway.

In short, an incredible life of decadence was forced upon the engineers and they loved every minute of it. Living well is the best revenge, so they say, and the Imagineers lived to the fullest – during those brief minutes of leisure afforded every week or so.

Any engineer staying at Fort Wilderness on a business trip relied heavily on the Meadow Trading Post as a source of dinner. Not being in Florida long enough to stock the refrigerator, and too tired to search out a dining establishment beyond the boundaries of the Fort, the unsuspecting engineer would seek out the Meadow Trading Post, to forage for the evening's meal. Upon surveying the various foods that they had selected for the frozen food section, the engineer would note that they hadn't selected anything that could be successfully prepared in a microwave oven, even though that was the type of oven in 90% of the trailers. This insuring that guests would be eating at one of the restaurants. Even the premium lines of frozen food had been pared down to "Macaroni in Tomato Sauce," or something equally horrible.

For a long while, if the engineers wanted to do any serious grocery shopping, it was necessary to drive fifteen miles to Kissimmee. Later, Goodings supermarket, perhaps the finest grocery store on Earth, was built on Sand Lake Road.

It's hard to convey the remoteness of Walt Disney World, before EPCOT was built, and the accompanying off-property building boom took place. It was really a forest when we first went down there, but the character of it really changed – apartments, hotels, shopping, even a new Civic Center.

Every night in Fort Wilderness at 10:00 o'clock one could hear the Sea Monster Music floating across the lagoon from the Electric Water Pageant. This would be followed by fireworks.

No matter how tired the engineers were, they all got a kick out of the same thing: "Here I am living in Walt Disney World. People are spending thousands of dollars to be here, and I'm living here." But living in Fort Wilderness with all the employees next to each other was very strange. It was like a family in some ways, but there was also a lot of hanky panky going on, and it was like Peyton Place, too. Sully was known to drive around the loop now and then, just to see who's car was parked where, and then tease them the next day: "So, you had a guest last night?" Soon though, the workload increased to the point that there was little time for any of that.

* * *

Linda was on relocation and Steve was on a business trip, and they were sharing a trailer. The relocation office just didn't know how to cope with that. So for a night or two they had two trailers. They had problems in the beginning because Disney didn't want the engineers to park two cars in one driveway. It was against regulations. They didn't want to turn the place into a parking lot. Finally, when the loop named Bobcat Bend became entirely WED employees, they gave up and let people park two cars at their trailers, but for a long while, one spouse had to park outside.

The Californians had always heard that in Florida they didn't have what it takes, and that Disneyland in Anaheim was where it was at. But Walt Disney World dwarfs Disneyland. Not only is the Magic Kingdom many times bigger, but there are whole themed resorts that form entities unto themselves, scattered across the 42 square miles of forest. At the first sight of the 18-story castle, even Disneyland begins to pale. Resorts, golf courses, theme parks, swimming pools, water slides.

On the back road from the Magic Kingdom into Fort Wilderness, there were almost always deer, raccoons, and families of bunnies outside the trailers. There were also armadillos. The Fort would have been filled with them, except that armadillos appear to have little of an animal's normal fear of highways. Ninety five percent of all the armadillos in the Fort seemed to be flat in the middle of the road.

Many engineers were terrified at the thought of trailers crawling with Palmetto bugs and scorpions. They had been told that critters were everywhere. Most of the stories were told to impress the folks back home, and even the relocation counselors were skittish when asked, "Exactly how *big* is a Palmetto bug, anyway?"

The counselors warned the engineers about the scorpions. But the stories that came back through the grapevine made those warnings sound like severe underestimations. "You've got to watch for the scorpions, there are scorpions all over the place, Sully was stung last week on the shoulder. The scorpions will get you." Linda found a scorpion in the bathtub. David found one when he walked into the bathroom carrying his shoes and dropped them on it, which didn't faze the scorpion at all. He immediately remedied that. Pound, pound, pound.

Engineers were told to watch out for water moccasins in the canal. There were banana spiders with four-inch leg spans in the backwoods behind the Fort. Like a lot of the Florida critters, the fact they were completely harmless made them no less terrifying.

When Rolando came home from work every day there were a dozen or more Palmetto bugs (basically, three-inch plus roaches) on the wall of his trailer next to the door. His wife would arrive home every day from running errands and would sit in the car and wait for him to get home.

Driving at night, on the back road between Fort Wilderness and the site, one's headlights often revealed hundreds of tiny tree frogs leaping across the road in the fog. It was as if there was life everywhere, almost a primordial atmosphere.

Spanish moss hung from almost every tree. Some felt it was romantic, the grey strands swaying in the breeze. Others felt differently. Phil said, "I can't live in a state where it continually smells like it's rotting. The whole state smells like it's rotting away".

* * *

The weather in Florida can be an experience in itself, especially to someone who grew up in California. Leaving the trailers (or coming home) early in the morning, there was fog unlike any in California – well-defined patches 10 feet wide and six feet high sitting a foot above the road.

Once, Andrew and David were out at Lake Buena Vista. They had been doing some shopping in the Village when they heard a storm warning on the radio. It hit within minutes. There was a tornado less than two miles away. They ran to the car, but the wind and rain were so intense that within a few feet they were soaked through. By the time they reached the car, the water in the parking lot was up to their ankles. David recalls, "We couldn't see more than five feet in front of the car. We were terrified in a way, but also having fun, sitting in the trailer with lightning striking so close that you could feel it before you heard it."

* * *

Every afternoon the storm clouds would build, and the sky would darken. One could literally feel the air ionizing. And then – crack! A bolt of lightning, and then another.

The radio dispatch office at EPCOT central monitored the weather radar and warned of approaching storm clouds or tornado activity, but the warnings didn't do much good. At the first lightning strike it was not uncommon for two or three pavilions to lose power, their computer control systems totally baffled by the sudden shortages or surges. At one point during the construction, a storm emptied over a foot of water into the American Adventure pit and did extensive damage all over the site. Miller Andress called a hasty meeting of all the resident engineers and chewed them out for not battening down the hatches at the first radio warning. From then on, anytime there was a storm warning within 20 miles of the property, everybody went running out and covered up all the exposed construction. It would take over a year before the computers became as storm-resistant as the structures.

Photos

Steve atop American Adventure at Epcot, July 1982. The unfinished theme park is in the background. Pretty scary: Not the height — the fact that it's only three months until opening!

Linda in front of a partly-covered Spaceship Earth. She was among the first engineers to make it to the site, and was ultimately responsible for the control systems in ten of the pavilions. And yes, it does look like Pacman.

Steve's fourth floor office in the Sun Bank building overlooking Lake Buena Vista and the Empress Lilly. We were given these luxurious offices, just one floor away from Dick Nunis' office, because the space had never been finished: Bare stud walls and concrete floors seemed fitting for engineers wearing construction garb. Still, we were an incongruous sight strolling across the lobby of the bank.

Epcot Central takes shape. A single tape binloop, and several cabinets were the first to arrive.

Italy under construction, June 1982.

France under construction, June 1982.

A lift on American Adventure being lowered into place with a construction crane.

Glenn next to one of the small lifts on American Adventure.

The Spaceship Earth downramp. John Ruck was continually frustrated by vehicles tearing audio equipment out of the track.

When the Porta-Potties got too dirty, the construction workers' solution was to set them on fire. This one they simply put up for sale. There weren't any takers.

After opening we moved to an office off of this tunnel under Communicore — opposite the garbage dumpster!

The Golden Paddle

It seemed as if he has barely shut his eyes when the alarm went off at 4:30 AM. In fact, his shift had ended at 2:00 AM. Without waking Linda, Steve quickly dressed in grubby cut-off shorts and an American Adventure tee shirt. He stepped outside into the muggy atmosphere of Fort Wilderness and climbed into his rental car. Past the sleeping trailers of Bobcat Bend in Fort Wilderness he drove, taking the back road through a card-key gate into the lush forest. A mother and four raccoons crossed the road in his headlights, and occasional patches of fog drifted by, barely 10 feet off the ground. In the early morning stillness he drove into the rear entrance of the Magic Kingdom. Leaving his car behind Big Thunder Mountain Railroad he entered the vacant streets of the sleeping park. The sun was just beginning to glow in the sky but already custodial and maintenance people were preparing for the day's guests, washing the pavement, waxing trash bins, polishing windows. At the lagoon he was greeted by other sleepy engineers; Ron Bittner, sacked out against a bench; Conrad, his voice more grave than usual; Walt, towering over all.

Soon the 10 engineers made their way down the ramp to the boarding area to select paddles and board a canoe. At the starting gun the paddles dug furiously into the water and the canoe lurched out onto the waterway. Past the rocky course, rounding Tom Sawyer Island, they headed for the home stretch. Walt, in a flurry, was virtually filling the boat with water, but the drenched Von sitting behind him didn't seem to mind, the water and air were both at least

80 degrees. At the finish line their time is read in the annual Walt Disney World canoe race.

The rules allow the last place teams to compete in sprint championships, while the faster teams compete in the finals. Enrollment is so small that the engineering team went on to win the sprint championship by being one of the slowest teams, and also took second place in the race.

The week after the finals the awards breakfast was held, early in the morning at the Crystal Palace on Main Street in the Magic Kingdom. The participants collected their award, a wooden paddle, painted gold, with their names on it. The name of the team was also inscribed on the paddle. It seemed appropriate for canoers who had spent so much time in the Pit of American Adventure. They called themselves "The Pit Crew".

Site Work

David recalls: My second or third day at EPCOT Walt had said "Dave, how you doing? Have you seen American Adventure yet?" I had said no, and he had offered to show me around. He had driven to the rear of the mammoth building. It looked just like all the other buildings at EPCOT from the rear, like a big warehouse. There was a light-trap door similar to the type in a photographic dark room, a makeshift thing made of plywood so that light wouldn't get inside and blind everyone when the door was opened.

It was completely dark inside the pavilion, just the light from the equipment. At first, I was completely blind. I knew there would be a guard there somewhere and I found a stairway railing at the entrance, so I grabbed hold of the railing for five or 10 minutes until I could see something.

When my eyes began to adjust to the inky blackness, I felt as if I were in a cavern. I could not see any of the walls, on the left or right. I was on a landing, elevated above the main floor. To the right was a pit that looked like it was a hundred feet deep. A huge black structure thrust up out of it, all metal and angular, things sticking out. I couldn't really tell what it was. If I had been asked my first impression I would have said it was an empty oil refinery or metal smelting plant.

Immediately in front of me was a staircase leading down to several rows of cabinets, with glowing indicators that provided the only discernible light. There was also a computer terminal and a serial logic analyzer where Bob was watching the data flowing between the ride control computers.

Standing by the railing of the pit as the carriage was going past was like standing on a dock when a large ship comes in. I couldn't feel any vibration and couldn't hear it. I had the sensation that the carriage was stationary and the whole building was moving.

Above me all I could see was scaffolding, catwalks, theater equipment, pulleys for the curtains, lighting, and a lot of rigging. The first place Walt took me was to one of the side equipment rooms, full of dimmers. From there we went up a spiral staircase to a catwalk about forty feet above the ground. Walt just walked right out onto it. I looked at the bottom of it, which was just a mesh, thinking 'Is this going to hold us?' Later I found out that was where they always took the first timers: up onto the mesh catwalk.

So we walked out onto the catwalk and when we got to the center Walt pointed everything out to me. 'That's the main carriage, that's the stage, that's where the curtains are going to be, that's where the audience is going to sit.' I looked at it and that was the first time at EPCOT that I was impressed with the size of something.

Then, he took me up onto the roof. Finally, after two years of working on something I could hardly imagine, there it was, stretched out in front of me. For the second time I felt, 'It really is pretty big.' And then I asked myself, 'How are we ever going to finish this?'"

The second morning after I arrived, Chris Senchack gave me some paperwork and said, "Go around to every pavilion and put one of these lists in each monitor cabinet." He felt it would be a good chance to learn the location of equipment on the site and immerse myself into the EPCOT I had so far only heard myths and legends about.

I also had to take a note of what paperwork was already in the monitor cabinets; this would mean finding each electronic equipment room on the site, locating the monitor cabinet among scores of nearly identical beige, six-foot tall boxes, and figuring out where some incorrigibly capricious engineer or tech had stashed whatever documentation was to be included in the cabinet. Had I known that some of the buildings weren't finished and most of the rooms were locked and most of the documentation was either still in

California or hidden deep within the recesses of the cabinet ("so it wouldn't get lost"), I would have told Chris to stick his head in the lagoon. But I didn't know any of that, and of course, neither did he. It was a fact-finding mission in more ways than one.

I started at 10:00 o'clock that morning, and whatever false impression I may have been given of the near-completeness of EPCOT was shot right to Hell before lunch. It was a typical, walking-through-a-rainforest-without-trees Florida day. I stumbled over piles of dirt and mud, dodged giant earthmovers and busloads of construction workers, stood in dumbfounded amazement at the giant cranes, slopped through puddles that were always six inches deeper than they looked and dragged myself through the stifling humidity and dust from unfinished building to unfinished building. The hum of the generators alone provided a small city's worth of noise. The din and energy level were near-nuclear. And over all, a fine dust, particles from every construction byproduct imaginable, settled on everything. The entire site smelled of diesel exhaust, wet plaster, freshly cut lumber and rotting swamp. I will forever associate those smells with EPCOT.

The site was also dangerous. For example, in a normal building, it is safe to assume when you approach a window on the fourth floor that there's going to be glass in it. At EPCOT though, you might find yourself standing on the edge of an unguarded precipice. Doors opened with no warning onto two- or three- story drops. With a push bar to open them! So you'd push open the door and whoosh... Your breath would vanish as you leaned into the abyss.

In short, to complete that three-hour chore, I worked from 10 o'clock, right through lunch and didn't return to the PICO Building until after 3:30 p.m.

I was more than somewhat humbled.

When I began the trek, I was optimistic in spite of the work I knew lay ahead. When I returned, it wasn't as if seeds of doubt were sown. No, it was more like I'd been hoed, uprooted, rototilled and moved aside by one of the earthmovers. I realized we had only three

81

months to finish. And Spaceship Earth was sitting in a mud hole, like a giant silver golf ball caught in an evil sand trap.

At least I was reassured by the atmosphere. Construction vehicles and burly men crawled over the site like human termites, moving earth and steel. And the site buzzed with electricity, not metaphorically, but literally, for everything was coordinated over walkie-talkie radios.

* * *

The radios chattered 168 hours a week, every week. Everything from technical questions, to locating someone for a meeting, to storm and tornado warnings. There was a special warning every time the Monorail beam was energized, because things were so crazy at the time, they could never tell who or what would be on it. Around opening day, radios were scarce. Everyone wanted to have one, although everyone said they were a pain in the ass. It was a status symbol to walk around with your flashlight and radio on your belt and your hardhat and steel-toed shoes.

But those radios were vital to getting any work done on the site.

There was even a rating system. They knew how long you'd been in Florida by what your call sign was. Conrad was 1 and Martin was 3. Glenn was 11 and Derek was 13. Walt was 20 and Bob Frye was 22.

Chris "stole" Electronics 2. It was John Noonan's call sign, but John had left Florida. When Chris arrived, he decided the number was prestigious and took it.

Ironically, numbers 14 and 15 were assigned to Jamie and Brian. They lived next to each other, both drove silver Datsun B210 wagons and had similar attitudes towards life. People kept on confusing them, and they often answered for each other on the radio since they often worked together. Conrad, who was their supervisor, was never quite sure who was who, even after Jamie and Brian had been there for a year and a half. One day, after he had finally gotten it straight, they switched name tags. That really blew his mind.

There were also humorous accidental and not-so-accidental transmissions. Jamie learned not to toss his radio onto the dash after he and Brian were greeted with strange looks at their next stop – they'd been broadcasting their opinions of the girls on the site as they drove. And one night, Derek had leaned back in a booth at Denny's, keying his radio during a detailed discussion with Sully about the merits of Penthouse Magazine.

Once, Steve, Linda and Glenn went to a lounge in Kissimmee and there was a dreadful cocktail singer. It was 11:30 at night and they decided that the rest of the site should hear it, so they started broadcasting.

* * *

Where did all the radio and construction and engineering activity radiate from? Where else?

From a half-empty warehouse.

That warehouse housed PICO, the Project Installation and Coordination Office. PICO was the official arm through which the engineers worked. It was the office that coordinated all activities, from Art Direction to Union Contractors.

PICO had a cement floor covered with the dirt from hundreds of pairs of dirty boots. Offices were unfinished rooms, just walls with tables and chairs thrown in at random. The electronics engineering office was downstairs in what was to become the women's locker room and part of the men's locker room.

Downstairs in the PICO Building was the main storage area. There was never a stranger room, filled with whole fiberglass bamboo roofs, double-decker buses, 15-feet high flowers and vines, lighting arrays and mysterious crates that came and went with no discernible pattern. On any given day, both plastic and real trees moved in and out.

At one point, it was decided to use the storage as a staging area to store the Energy vehicles, moving platforms containing one hundred movie theater seats, but unfortunately the roll up door was a foot and a half too narrow, so they had to cut a tiny swinging door out of the side of the big door.

In spite of all this chaos, or perhaps because of it, working for PICO was considered a prestige position among Walt Disney World employees.

Well, actually there was good reason. Unlike the rest of the Disney empire, Employees of WED and the Studio are not bound by the Disney dress code, which required hair cut above the ears and neck and no facial hair for men; limited jewelry and make-up for women; neat dress at all times.

As the PICO offices became overrun by WED West people, it became easy to spot an Ex-Californian. He was the only one in the employee cafeteria with long hair and a face that hadn't been shaved in a week.

The American Adventure crew had it even luckier than the rest of PICO. Steve remembers: "We acquired the Sun Bank Offices with the beautiful view overlooking Lake Buena Vista Village, and in this completely unfinished office with a cement floor and metal stud walls we designed American Adventure. Every morning, we'd go into this beautiful bank in our grimy, grease-soaked jeans that we'd been working in all night, our noisy radios strapped to our belts and a bag full of parts and a hard hat under our arms. We'd line up with all the people in their business suits to wait for the elevator.

"We were spoiled and we were completely autonomous. That's the only way we got the job done. Having all of those people working those ridiculous hours."

* * *

The general attitude expressed by the dress and grooming of the average male WED California employee was, "Who gives a shit what I look like? I'm sacrificing just being here!" The women were only slightly more conscious of their looks than the men, but after a little while on the site, most of them began looking a LOT more casual than they ever had in California.

The "sacrificing myself to a higher cause" look made the WED transplants highly conspicuous to the construction workers, who looked upon the engineers as college brats with too many brains who worked too many hours. The underlying attitude of the average transplant, which was not lost at all among the construction workers, was that a WEDI could, if he or she wanted to, complete the work of a squadron of union men in a single evening.

With the reaction of men who fear the loss of their jobs, many responded with unbridled hostility towards PICO. Not just slow cooperation or catcalls for the women, but derisive chanting, "PICO...PICO...PICO..." In closer quarters, it was a threatening, sotto voce, "Fuckin' PICO," giving the impression that after work, college boy, it's you and me — and, of course, my buddies.

Most of the engineers played along or made friends or just avoided burly men wearing jeans and tattoos.

As hard as the men had it, the WED women had it tougher. In addition to being ex-Cals, they had to put up with the rampant sexism on the construction site. Whistles, cat calls, propositions and just the good ol' boy attitude of "What's a nice li'l girl like you doin' in a tough place like this?" could be expected on a daily basis, especially in the early days. There were a number of women on the site including Jenny Atwood, Linda Alcorn, June DiRienzo, Francie Owen, Jane Jackson, Nancy Gee Bugman, Melanie Simon, Phronie Sanders and others.

Linda remembers how it was to acclimate to the overwhelmingly male environment: "In the beginning they were unsure if they wanted to send me down at all. I think there was some concern about sending somebody who wasn't quite 5'2" into the midst of all that. Lee was nervous about it a little bit; on the other hand, it finally got to the point where he simply had no choice. As it was, it turned out okay.

"I learned a lot of rules real quick. Women were not allowed to wear skirts on the site, we had to wear pants of some sort. We could not walk anywhere along a road without being whistled at and having things yelled at us. I quickly learned that there were two categories of that; sort of jovial hellos and then the other kind. I really only felt that I had something yelled at me once that was offensive. The rest of the time it was just guys being guys, but it wasn't meant to be insulting. I felt that if you were going to get upset about being whistled at you simply had no business on that site."

After Linda had been on-site for awhile somebody came up behind her driving a truck. She could hear it idling behind her and a guy started screaming "Hey baby, why don't you hop in?" She didn't look around because she was afraid it was some really obnoxious construction worker. When she finally glanced around and looked it was Brian Cox. He was only joking, but it underscored the general atmosphere on the site for the women. They had to be prepared to handle just about anything.

Gradually, most of those women engineers were accepted. Although some were never well-liked, others functioned perfectly well and were quite comfortable on the construction site working with the construction workers. But there was a startling contrast between the women engineers and the few female construction workers on the site who were real rednecks. Like the female welder character in the American Adventure show, they were tough.

After months of working on the site, there were fewer and fewer gender distinctions. Anyone was accepted if they pulled their weight.

Linda remembers: It was very dirty. I remember stepping in mud up to my ankles on several occasions and construction workers laughing at me for that. I also remember that if you wanted any respect you couldn't really do anything that would be considered "feminine." One time I wrenched my ankle really badly in front of five or six guys with whom I was working. I got up and I started walking. I was in considerable pain but they were amazed that I walked. I think I got some points from that. I think they expected me to dissolve. But not walking wasn't really one of my options at that point.

Mostly I was doing just what the guys were. I was supervising the installation of equipment, making sure that things were connected properly, and turning them on and verifying that all the connections went back where they were supposed to.

It was vital to get in good with the electrical foreman on the job, gain his confidence and make him understand that you were there to do your job; that you weren't trying to do his. You also had to get in good with his top guys. Frequently I found that I was assigned guys to work with me who were good. They were interested in doing a good job and they weren't real rednecks in the sense that they wouldn't work with or for a woman. As long as I respected them they respected me.

Lots of times, you could get away with murder after a little while if you knew the foreman and you said "Look, this is wrong in this back room, is the world going to fall apart if I just quickly slip in there and rewire this?" He'd just turn around and walk away and you knew that you could get away with it.

* * *

One of the perks of being sent to Florida was getting a rental car. The company was really good about that, since they could have leased a bunch of rent-a-wrecks, or made people share cars, or even just rented bicycles of golf carts; after all, we were supposed to spend all our waking hours working towards The Goal. Who would have the time or energy to drive anywhere?

Of course, the company didn't look at it that way (fortunately). And of course, like everything else, they went first class (double-fortunately).

Those people who were relocated had their choice of several nice subcompact cars (usually Datsuns) and even some economy wagon/hatchbacks. People who were on business trips, for some reason, got full-size cars. For married employee, this usually meant a Buick, Pontiac or even a Cadillac.

For single employees, it meant one thing – a sports car.

Fort Wilderness was filled with Camaros, Firebirds, Celicas and other fast rides being driven by employees with one purpose in life: to disobey every traffic law under the sun while driving on Disney property.

Speed limits became meaningless; no-parking zones unheard of; traffic signals might as well have been lamp posts. No law was sacred and many a shuttle bus driver on the Fort Wilderness road was startled by the sight of a low, mean, racing machine bearing down on a bus load of tourists at full throttle, veering off and passing the turtle-slow vehicle *on the wrong side of the street*, then pulling back in just in time to avoid hitting a Winnebago taking two families from Atlanta home from their Disney experience. All, of course, taking place around a blind corner in a 5 MPH zone.

No matter how much one respected the law in Los Angeles, no matter how many automatic license renewals one had received, no matter how many good driver citations one had received from the local police, no matter how hard one tried to be good, arriving in Florida turned you into a speed demon, a hell-blasting thrill freak.

The general attitude was, "There are no real cops on the property, who's going to arrest me? This is not my car, it's a rental and it's insured. Do you think they really expect anyone not to pass the shuttle buses?"

The people at National said that at one time in the Summer of '82, Disney had rented almost 200 cars from them. They were bringing in cars from New Orleans and every major city in the area.

Brian Cox used to say, "They're not rent-a-cars, they're *dent-a-cars*."

The National and American International car rental agencies in Orlando would no doubt concur. Only a few accountants know how much auto insurance added to the cost of building EPCOT, or how many customers ended up stranded 30 miles east of Kissimmee when the transmission fell out of a car previously rented by a WED engineer.

Accidents on the property were many. And for those employees who forgot to turn off their on-site attitude in the real world, so were tickets. Matters weren't helped much when an article in the Sunday magazine of the Orlando Sentinel quoted the chief of the highway patrol as saying they didn't have the manpower, time nor inclination to stop anybody traveling at less than 65 MPH. (The speed limit was 55 at the time.)

But the very best part of it all was that the company paid for all the gas.

Nightlife

Florida nightlife was perhaps unlike any other in the world. Where else could you have a clean, family, Disney experience, check out an expensive French restaurant, get down-home Southern fried food, visit bars where a $5 cover gets you all you can drink, and cap off the week by having a half-naked woman buck around on your lap as if you were a mechanical bull?

And that's just from Monday to Friday. As for the weekends... Well!

Of course, entertainment in the Disney complex was all as clean as the proverbial whistle, cleaner perhaps. There was the Top of the World show at the Contemporary Resort, a crisp and entertaining revue/review of great Broadway musicals, featuring kids with a tad more talent than is common around the park.

Then, at Fort Wilderness, there was the Hoop de Doo Revue, more what you expect from Disney: a foot-stompin', deep-fried dance/vaudeville extravaganza as southern as fried chicken – and as unchallenging to the palette.

There was a Polynesian luau thing over at the Polynesian Resort.

And, of course, there was the usual Disney contingent of shows, on-the-spot performances, fireworks, music and comedy, not to mention the myriad of fair to middling Disney cuisine dished out at the legion of restaurants and stands scattered about the property. They say Disney's Florida property is as big as Manhattan. It seems to have as many places to eat.

After a while, though, any on-site entertainment or food was routinely avoided by any but the most pixie-dusted employee, or those with a constant stream of visitors all waiting to be taken "around the world."

(This is before EPCOT opened, bringing "real" food to the parks for the first time. Of course, this was no secret, and employees went to town rather than suffer the high prices and difficult reservation system of these overcrowded venues.)

Instead, the employees often left the property in search of better, wilder and more escapist fare. They didn't have to look far.

Adjacent to the lobby of the Royal Plaza Hotel was a bar named the Giraffe. Although it was actually on Disney property, it was outside of Disney jurisdiction. There was nothing remarkable about the bar, except during "happy hour," from 4 to 6 p.m., when drinks were two for the price of one, and hors d'oeuvres were free. To some ex-Californians, looking for escape from EPCOT's pressures and some fast food to stuff down their gullet, happy hour provided an irresistible package.

So they made their way to the Giraffe. The bar was quite a scene on Thursday night, payday, with happy hour going full swing. The place was so packed, you'd have to be a giraffe to see over all the Disneyites in their Izod shirts, construction workers with their muscular arms bulging from tee shirts, and hotel guests in polyester Mickey Mouse shirts wondering "Where in all Hell is this crazy mix of people coming from. I mean, are they staying here?"

In the midst of this, soaking it in like sunshine, were the California engineers, with their wild hair and oily blue jeans, exuding their, "Who gives a shit what I look like? I'm sacrificing just being here!" look. Their only concession to style was the careful removal of the Disney name tag before entering. The company considers it "bad show" to be seen as part of the consuming, er, imbibing, public while wearing your badge – and no matter how irreverent the employee, that's one rule that no one cares to mess with. (Besides, the little Mickey Mouse on the badge cramps your style.)

During the summertime, there were nightly trips to the Giraffe for sustenance.

With its hyped-up atmosphere, it's no surprise that the Giraffe was the birth site of what became a notorious and nasty union/ management incident.

A union worker was taken out for a "break" one night by a PICO engineer, a WED employee. The WED employee was off for the night, but for the union guy it was only a lunch break. On this particular night, the engineer and the union man seated themselves at the bar. The union man decided to show the engineer how a Real Man drank, and proceeded to polish off a few ounces of hard booze. When the bartender caught on to the sheer endurance of the two-fisted drinker at the bar that night, he started providing free liquid fire, just to see what the Man was made of.

After gulping down what witnesses argue was 10 to 20 shots of Kentucky lightning or Alabama hardjack, the union man got up and...didn't fall flat on his face, as all had expected. Impressed, the engineer drove him back to work, where the Man... was found dead-drunk and out cold in the back of a pick-up truck the next morning.

He was summarily fired, but not before a howl went up for equal time – the union guys wanted the PICO guy fired for his part in the crime, or they would walk off the job. So management stepped in and hauled the engineer back to California until things cooled down. A week later the union man was back on the job under a different sub-contractor on a different pavilion.

Sleazier things may have happened further from the site, but news of them didn't drift back very often. No doubt, many infamous events took place about 15 miles off-property, on Orlando's famous South Orange Blossom Trail, a.k.a. the SOBT.

The SOBT is Orlando's red light district – sort of. It is a strange mixture of shopping malls, decent restaurants, hotels, banks and sleazy, sleazy, sleazy, sleazy adult entertainment. It was the sort of place you would never expect to find a Disney employee, but it was the Pixie Dust addict's equivalent of a methadone fix, and many of the single (and some of the married) ex-Cals made the trail a decompression stop on the way home from the pressure of the job.

If you were married, chances were that you missed out on a lot of the things that the single people were doing. When one engineer (Scott A.) came out, he had a little crew that spent almost every other night out on the "Trail". David remembers waking up one morning to find his car plastered with bumper stickers from the Doll House, a favorite male hangout. He knew that the "trail crew" had done it.

Sooner or later, most of the ex-Cal men knew about the Doll House. It was a topless bar and lunch buffet that had the prime position on the SOBT – it was the first strip joint on the way out of Disney property, less than 15 miles from the park.

Unlike strip bars in Los Angeles and many other metropolitan areas, the Doll House was not a dumping ground for drug addicts, ex-whores and other unfortunate women. Like everything else in Orlando, it had, ironically, a Disney touch of fantasy. The women could all be Playboy centerfold candidates and the place was as clean and polite as any restaurant on Disney property. There was even complementary popcorn.

For the price of admission, one or two dollars, adult men wearing anything from a manager's suit and tie to a construction worker's overalls could sit and watch pretty young women shake their naked flesh to the latest and loudest in contemporary pop music.

Needless to say, the place was always packed.

Down the street, almost at the other end of the trail, for the women, was Park Avenue West. A disco most nights and a punk hangout Wednesdays, the club offered Chippendales-type male dancers on Mondays.

Needless to say, the place was always packed.

Less likely to be packed, but still visited by some ex-Cal men, were the more "adult" types of entertainment that peppered the strip between the Doll House and Park Avenue. There were 25c movie theaters, adult bookstores and nude bars, where (rumor has it) the women who were unfit for the Doll House were employed.

Then there were the places that offered lap dancing.

Lap dancing was an entirely new concept to most ex-Californians, because lap dancing was illegal in most of California. Lap dancing is when a woman, in various stages of dress or undress, straddles a seated, fully clothed man and wiggles her seated area upon his lap for the length of one song on a juke box. The woman may be wearing a gown, a bathing suit, just the bottom of a bathing suit, or (supposedly, many years ago) nothing.

In some places, the lap dances take place in the main room of the bar, in full view of the other customers. In others, patrons were led to an outside room, for a little privacy.

In California at the time, lap dancing was legally considered prostitution. In Florida, some say it's good clean fun, although the Orlando city council had a vendetta against the red light district because it tarnished the city's image for tourists.

To say that some ex-California men were intrigued by lap dances is an understatement, but let's leave it at that: Food for thought.

Speaking of food, this is a good point to talk about food. Most of the ex-Californians had been living off of the food from the Lake Buena Vista employee cafeteria for months. At first, it was the only place near the site to get a decent meal. In the summer of '82, the company finally opened an employee cafeteria in the still-under-construction Canada pavilion, so the food service employees could practice serving food in the restaurant. Unfortunately, it was still the same food. Then there was the regular on-site grub shop that would eventually become the main employee cafeteria when EPCOT opened. It was also still the same food, only worse.

When employees couldn't take it any more, they'd go "off property" to get food, even junk food. The problem with Disney food was not that it was bad, it was that after a while, it all tasted the same. It was remarkably consistent, as much as McDonald's.

The nearest places to get "real" food were Kissimmee and International Drive. International Drive offered a variety of restaurants, including Bennigan's and People's, the two most popular lunch and dinner hangouts. Bennigan's served something called Banana Banshees, incredible drinks that had absolutely no alcohol in them at all – that you could taste. They seemed a safe lunch break drink. Big mistake.

Linda remembers that around the middle of July it really got pretty intense and for the most part she did not leave the property except late at night. At 10:00 o'clock or so, she'd make a quick trip out to Taco Bell in Kissimmee, rather than eat more food from the employee cafeterias.

Late night trips were the rule more than the exception. It was not uncommon to work around the clock without eating at all, then break off at 10 p.m. or midnight or 2 in the morning and head into town for a late meal, a nightcap or even a little action on the SOBT. Sleep was something that often fell between 4 a.m. and noon. (Even 6 a.m. to 2 p.m. was not abnormal.)

Fortunately, Orlando is a tourist/convention town, so there are a lot of places to grab a bite. Ex-Cals' stomachs simply lost any pretension to natural clocks, schedules or regular appetites. Like POWs, they simply became accustomed to taking whatever small morsels were available at any time they were offered.

For the real die-hard, it was a fortunate fact that 7-Elevens in Orlando are almost as common as gas stations in Los Angeles, so in moments of real desperation one could always whip up some Twinkies, Fritos or even (if you were crazed enough to remember you had a kitchen) a real *meal*.

* * *

Strangely enough, when a spare moment was to be found, the ex-Cals often spent it doing what they normally did back home. The tourist stuff, which all but surrounded them, could only be exciting for so long, then it was back to the familiar patterns of shopping, movies, concerts and picnics in the park.

Movies, for one thing, could be a very different experience in Orlando than Los Angeles. In spite of its reputation, Los Angeles, home of almost every wild form of entertainment known to man, doesn't have cinema pubs.

Cinema pubs are simply a logical extension of the Sunday afternoon/Saturday night TV/beer party. Except instead of staying home, you visit the local theater. The TV is exchanged for a big screen and the beer is supplemented by wine, chips and sandwiches. And the price of admission: one or two dollars. Of course, the CPs were often packed with rowdy moviegoers willing to see a slightly less than first run movie in exchange for being able to see the film with an expanded consciousness.

Several ex-Cals expressed a desire to bring the CPs back home and enlighten the populace, but for one reason or another, it never happened. Suburbs like Chatsworth would never be the same again.

Isolated from the world in $95 a night campsites, few of the relocated Imagineers seemed to care as the hours crept up to 60, 70, 80 or more each week. Their disbelieving counterparts back in California smiled and shook their heads at the 100-hour time sheets. "Now really, how many hours did you work last week?"

What mattered was that we were "Out here," in the big mud hole that would soon attract millions. The running joke was, "I hear we get to work half-days next week." To which one replied, "Yeah, twelve hours a day." The Great Scimitar of Opening Day drew closer and jokes became rarer. It's hard to be funny after working 26 hours straight with no sleep, and no food since lunch a day ago.

Nobody seemed to notice the affect this all was having on these kids, who were humping the great mud hole for all it was worth, sweating and organizing and somehow making things fall from chaos into order, putting in unbelievable hours for weeks at a time. Away from their homes, families, friends, and reality.

Underlying it all was a frenetic feeling, a sense of this massive project hanging from an ever-decreasing number of slender threads.

Life in the Pit

It was 3:00 o'clock in the morning on a steamy July day in the Pit of American Adventure. Construction dust left from the previous day's frenzied activities in the rafters slowly filtered its way to the floor, seventy feet below. Two engineers, Glenn and Steve, crouched near a row of cabinets, probing the circuits with a variety of test equipment. Down near the bottom of the Pit, Frank, a technician, re-wires a cabinet by the light of a flashlight. Every hour or two his screwdriver would slip from his fingers and bounce through the maze of metal scaffolding, solenoids and hydraulic pistons to land in a pool of hydraulic oil 14 feet below. Construction workers crawled about, adjusting valves and retrieving lost screwdrivers. These were the third shift workers in a building that never slept.

Lighting equipment was being installed in the rafters and catwalks at various altitudes in the theater. Special effects projectors would soon be creating stars, sunrises and ticker tape effects. Out in the theater, seats had not yet been installed, but air conditioning ducts thrust up between each position, and mounting bolts were already in place. The walls of the theater were still in an unfinished state, with plasterboard and tape strewn here and there. The theater ceiling, which was being plastered, could be reached only through a maze of scaffolding.

The theater and stage were separated by a gigantic asbestos curtain, lowered to keep the construction dirt in the theater away from the supposedly cleaner environment of the stage area. Metalwork was being installed across the top and bottom of the stage to support the rear projection screen, which would soon stretch

180 feet from side to side. Below it the top of the large carriage was visible. This steel behemoth rolls from underneath the audience to position 10 lifts – some weighing up to 60,000 pounds – in the proper spot to rise at the front of the stage. A smaller carriage carrying one lift and a raft that hinges down off the front, rolls from the right of the stage out to a position that places the raft above the large carriage. Interlocks are being installed to prevent the raft from crashing into the large carriage if it is hinged down.

Steve and Glenn soon became accustomed to debugging sophisticated electronic computers with welding sparks falling all around them, while people cursed at the welders who were dropping the molten stuff. Mountains of dirt blew in through the loading door as the construction workers moved set pieces in to install them on lifts. Every day or two it became necessary to take the circuit boards out of the computers and blow them off so that they could tell that there were any parts on them at all.

The supposed "dust-free date" had long since passed, but a shovel still seemed more appropriate than a broom. Several cabinets had malfunctioned because there was so much dirt on the boards that when the humidity got high it shorted out the components.

Because it was a union environment the engineers could not legally wire or rewire anything themselves. Instead, they were required to direct the efforts of union labor. Often games were played to obtain a cooperative union worker who would stand by twiddling his thumbs while the engineers did the work using his tools.

There were two different major contractors involved in each pavilion. One was the general contractor, who was different for each building. Tishman was the overall contractor for all of EPCOT and supervised all the general contractors. The general contractors had myriad subcontractors who came and went as different jobs were required: cement, electrical, roofing, paint, plumbing and so on.

The other major contractor that engineers were involved with was the Disney-owned Buena Vista Construction Company, known as BVCC.

The rumor was that it was very difficult to work with the general contractors because they were interested in making a profit, weren't very helpful, and their union people were interested in making the job last as long as possible, sometimes to the point of resorting to sabotage. It was supposedly easier to work with BVCC since that was Disney-owned.

So there was a great impetus to get things bought off as quickly as possible. It was a strange situation, with the customer, Disney, saying, "Yes, you've completed the job the way that you contracted to, and you may go now," while the contractor was fighting to convince Disney that they hadn't yet satisfactorily finished so that they would have more work.

This "buying off" was done on a very microscopic scale in some pavilions, such as American Adventure. There, individual lifts were bought off one at a time. Once those lifts were bought off, it was easier for the engineers to work with the equipment even though BVCC still had rules that theoretically prevented them from doing any electrical work.

To get anything done in American Adventure it was necessary to start high in the hierarchy of contractors, usually with Jerry Mick from Tishman. He would then talk to the general contractor, Darrin and Armstrong, who would then talk to the boss for the electrical subcontractor, Paxson. He would then talk to his foreman, who would then talk to the lead. Finally the lead would assign one of his workers. Usually it was somebody who looked like the only electrical work they had ever done was plugging in a television. Usually they were assigned to some fairly delicate work, since many of the computer cabinets hadn't even been completely wired when they were shipped. There is nothing quite as frightening to an engineer working on a delicate computer as an electrician holding a pair of 18" electrician's cutters waiting to be told how to install jumpers on a circuit board.

The American Adventure show was ready for animation figure programming in July. In the theater a programmer's console, created by Department 510, was set up. The console showed a picture of a figure, with knobs installed at anatomical joints to control the movement. The console was actually a sophisticated computer that communicated to EPCOT Central, where a Show Control Unit, another 510 creation, generated the animation data. Each moment of the show could be stepped slowly forward and back, while the position of a figure's limbs was slightly altered. It was a laborious process that took weeks to complete. The figures were already programmed once at the Tujunga building, but they behaved slightly differently after being installed, and had to be fine-tuned. In addition, all those things that could not be programmed in Tujunga needed to be entered into the computer, including curtains, lighting and dozens of audio channels.

Davey and Rick sat at the console, manipulating the knobs that controlled Ben Franklin until they were happy with the way the figure climbed the stairs in the second scene. Bit by bit, over the weeks that followed, Davey began to achieve a dynamic and sympathetic relationship between the various figures never before seen in an audio-animatronics show. These figures were far more complex than in any other Disney show, some of them having nearly a hundred individual controls. To complicate matters, the figures behaved differently at different speeds or when several movements occurred in conjunction with one another. If a torso turn was altered it often was necessary to re-program the arm joint as well.

Dennis Manley fell in American Adventure. He slipped on hydraulic oil and broke several ribs. He went home to California, only to return in a couple of months. Almost the first day he was back, he and Mark Meier were driving past one of the huge earth graders, the biggest pieces of equipment on the Site, just as it turned into the Germany back area. The car was demolished, and Dennis' arm was broken.

The Great Scimitar

David describes his first months at EPCOT: Everyone warned me when I hired into Disney, "You're a wirelister, so you get blamed for everything that goes wrong." I think of all the wirelists that we did, all the thousands and thousands of lines of information, the number of mistakes we made was probably less than 1-1/100th of 1%. But sure enough, as soon as I got to Florida, I found that the technicians and the MAPO people were distressed with the wirelists. Not because they had errors, but because the cabinets had been redesigned in the field without the wirelists being updated. But they blamed the wirelisters. As far as I know, most of the wirelists are still useless. You never know what to expect when you look at one of those cabinets.

I remembered that I had heard all about the Retreat. I'd ask people, "Why do they call it the Retreat?" They would just laugh. "You'll know when you go there." Driving out to it with Ken, it was way the hell away from anything. I found out that that was why they called it the Retreat, not because it was plush or anything. I remember thinking, "What the hell can they accomplish out here?"

It was probably the only run-down area in all of Walt Disney World. It looked like a cheap trailer park somewhere outside of Reno. Inside it was piled with equipment. There were microcomputer development systems and a couple of halfway-torn-apart monitor cabinet computers, with wires all over the place. There was a bench in the back that was covered with parts and drawers and little pieces of electronic parts.

I was astounded, that a run-down trailer with peeling paint, decaying wood and a carpet that smelled like mildew would contain $100,000 worth of electronics.

But that was where it was happening. Bit by bit the gang at the Retreat was bringing to life the software that would be needed to run EPCOT in just a few short weeks.

I'd find Mark working for thirty-six hours living on Twinkies and cans of Coke. Jamie would be there working thirty, forty hours straight. Amazingly, they'd still be producing. Occasionally one would jump up and shout, "Aha! I've found the problem." I came to think after awhile that the Retreat was the heart and soul of EPCOT, because I started to feel so strongly about the software effort for the show and monitor systems. I thought "This is EPCOT, this is the think tank of EPCOT." They worked as if they were on a mission from God.

Rolando and Andrew would be trying to get new sections of the monitor cabinet code to work. When the right lights in the test equipment came on they would scream and jump up and down, rocking the trailer.

I am still amazed at how young the Retreat gang was. Greg and Ken and Andrew were all barely into their twenties. They were given immense responsibilities and a lot of independence, and they pulled it off. I once watched Greg condense a couple of pages of badly written software into eight lines in less than fifteen minutes. Software he had never seen before.

I remember learning the monitor cabinet software tables in three days. It was unlike anything I'd ever done before. It took me a week to do my first cabinet, but by the time it got to scrambling for opening day, I was doing three cabinets a day, trying to get out monitor software for whatever I could, revising it, re-revising it. I remember the constant pressure. I went from a paper-pusher entering tables to going out in the field and acting as a technician, almost overnight. I remember sitting with Jim Robinson by a monitor cabinet with a switch box, checking each point out, watching the lights light up on the monitor cabinet cards, and feeling both shocked and ecstatic by the progress we were all making.

* * *

World of Motion was a General Motors-sponsored ride which traces the history of transportation from foot power to the world of the future. It was the first ride to be finished by art direction, and the first to be engineered. As show engineer, Linda had to break much new ground and write many specs in an attempt to achieve some level of standardization between this and all other rides. There are more animated figures in World of Motion than in any show that Disney had ever done before, and although their movements were relatively simple, just keeping track of every person, dog, chicken and horse was a major effort. The ride is long, 18 minutes, and there are many scenes. Each had to be individually programmed, lit and controlled. Because it was the first, it would also be used to train the Operations people until the other rides were ready.

Linda recalls: One day we decided to bring up the footprint control cabinet in World of Motion. It was responsible for handling all of the lights that slowly faded on and off in footprints that walked on the cave man's wall. We examined the whole thing and it all looked like it was in pretty good shape. We checked out some of the wiring to the footprints, and then powered the thing up. After about 10 or 15 seconds there was suddenly a "Pop!" "Well, gee, I wonder what that was?" Suddenly there was another "pop" and then "pop, pop, pop!" We noticed a bunch of burnt cotton flying out of the front of the cabinet from in-between the boards. "What the hell is going on here?" "Pop, pop, pop!" We switched the breaker off and looked in. Dozens of capacitors in the cabinet had exploded, throwing burnt cotton all over the boards. Later we determined that the power was applied across them backwards.

Once, they pulled out a board and found a dead dragonfly on it.

* * *

In the France pavilion the five reels of film arrived from the studio in Burbank and were loaded into the projectors. A variety of construction workers, art directors and off duty engineers gathered for the first showing of the film. As the opening scenes rolled it quickly became apparent that one of the five projectors had not started, so that the scenery had a hole in it, but the audio clarity impressed everyone, even in its un-tweaked state. The low notes rumbled through the theater, vibrating the seats, while the high notes tinkled with a crystal-like clarity. It was obviously a much better sound system than anyone had heard in a Disney theme park before. Unfortunately, it was so good that the lisp of the narrator, unheard in the recording studio, was quite apparent. The narration had to be re-recorded.

* * *

Often it was necessary to experiment to find the your way across the site. Road construction (and destruction) was an ongoing process. Sometimes it was a challenge, or even an impossibility, to get where you wanted.

Driving through mounds of dirt and pools of mud underneath Spaceship Earth before West CommuniCore Construction had begun, one got the distinct impression of a cross-country road rally. The drive through Future World was a drive through mounds of dirt and mud holes; you competed with the large tractors in order to get through. Driving under Spaceship Earth was like off-road racing.

One day, somebody in front of Glenn slowly drove a car down into the mud. Glenn had to call Security to get them towed out.

The only way to get through some obstacles was to floor the gas pedal, get the car up to 50 or 60 miles an hour, and plow through with enough momentum to get to the other side.

There were hills of dirt and debris as far as the eye could see (usually about a hundred feet). And rising out of it were the pedestal legs that Spaceship Earth rested on. The only approach was to abandon the car amidst the heavy earth moving equipment, hoping that there wouldn't be a mountain there when you returned. Overhead, dozens of workers marched up and down carrying set pieces. Spaceship Earth was into set installation at that point, but the track was not in through a lot of the ride. They started at the top and worked down. Inside it was absolutely filthy.

The general inconvenience of Spaceship Earth was amazing. It was a building 18 stories tall that for the most part could only be accessed through a set of stairs that crossed the track in a couple of places. One had to walk out one door and across the track to another door to continue up the stairs. There was a steep, steel ramp on either side of the track. Walking up and down Spaceship Earth a few times a day left little energy for anything else. Sometimes the unwary visitor would climb all the way to the top, only to find the doors on every landing locked. Later a service elevator was put in, but it doesn't go all the way to the top.

When the ride was energized the first time, the clamor of grinding metal and straining tires demonstrated the inability of the drive system to lift the massive load. The Spaceship Earth ride is driven by slowly rotating tires mounted in the track. These wheels push against the bottoms of the vehicles, forcing them up a steep, winding grade 180 feet high. When they pass the crest they wind down an even steeper grade to the bottom.

All of the vehicles are linked together with tow bars to form an endless chain, so all of the motors must be started at the same moment in order to get the chain moving. When the ride was designed, the number of motors required to perform this Herculean feat was underestimated by a considerable percentage. Installing additional motors meant removing some of the cars and disconnecting some of the equipment in the track, including the audio power bus bar. The audio system would never be the same.

* * *

The Land pavilion has many different attractions within one structure. One is an animated show called Kitchen Kabaret in which vegetables and fruits sing and dance in a gigantic kitchen. Although no one expected much from this corny (no pun intended) concept, it proved amusing in its test show at Tujunga and everyone was anxious to see it operating in the art deco theater for which it was designed. Another attraction in Land is the Harvest Theater, a 70 millimeter film to be shown in a theater that is too steep and difficult to load crowds rapidly.

The Land also contains one of the major dining areas in World Showcase, including The Good Turn restaurant, which revolves through farms, deserts and jungles. There is also a "Farmer's Market," a food court where many small booths would sell salads, sandwiches and ice cream. In July of 1982, it looked more like a giant shopping mall.

Adjacent to the dining area is the loading area for the Land boat ride. "Listen to the Land." Here visitors would ride computer-controlled boats in a canal, through greenhouses where new cultivation techniques would be demonstrated. When it was time to test the ride, the canal was filled with water and it quickly became apparent that the water level wasn't high enough to float the boats. It was also quickly discovered that it does not take a half a dozen computers to control boats floating through a trough.

* * *

Circle Vision Theaters are a mainstay of World Showcase. China and Canada both contain these circular theaters, and France contains a semi-circle. The design of each is similar. Seats or lean rails are provided for guests on the ground floor. Automatic doors are cycled by show control equipment and governed by hydraulic pumps hidden somewhere on the ground floor. Overhead, a projection room encircles the entire theater, behind the screens. Nine projectors and their associated control cabinets are hidden in the gaps between the screens. Each projector is fed with film from a film loop cabinet, where the celluloid winds from reel to reel-to-reel, never coming into contact with itself. Tiny peepholes, too small to serve any purpose whatsoever, afford a view of a minuscule portion of the opposing screen. Audio equipment is in another room, downstairs.

Invariably, it would be necessary to reset two cabinets connected intimately together. Logically, the cabinets were located in rooms that were twenty feet away – as the electric drill flies. This often turned out to be a 10-minute walk by human footpower. This was particularly true in China, where three locked, auto-closing doors separated two cabinets which had to be reset within 45 seconds of each other.

* * *

In Energy, the guests are loaded into the show to view a movie, but at the end of the movie, they discover they are seated in six vehicles that hold a hundred or more people each. The vehicles are powered by solar electricity and guided by radio signals from wires imbedded in the concrete. All six vehicles position themselves on a large turntable. The turntable rotates so that the vehicles can enter a prehistoric valley, complete with full-sized dinosaurs and smelly mist.

* * *

With opening day so close, one did not know what changes to expect in the engineers' mental stability. The worst-case scenario included an epidemic of Pixie Dust panic, with engineers working around the clock for a week, out in the field with equipment that refused to work. Laborers would become just as uncooperative as the equipment, intimidating the engineers with threats of union reprisal if they so much as touched a screwdriver. The underfed, overworked engineers would scream out for nourishment and rest, afraid that if management saw them going home to sleep, they will be accused of having fun.

Then, when it was all over, management, in a fit of pique over the cruel humor the engineers exhibited in drawing things out until the last minute, would fire each and every one of them.

That worst-case scenario is surprisingly close to what happened.

There were an optimistic few who believed from the beginning that EPCOT would open on time. But even the pessimists greatly underestimated the superhuman effort it would take to pull it off.

So each Imagineer began to feel the effects of a Pixie Dust panic, an adrenalin surge that lasted nearly three months. It was a surge powered by raw nerves, and the knowledge that heads were on the block. "The project is in your hands, kids."

Personalities began to change. Tempers flared, relationships snapped, and yet things got done. The great snafu crouched, ready to pounce, yet was held at bay. The vice-president cried. The construction foremen, contractors, and veteran engineers couldn't believe that a bunch of college kids could make it happen, but they did, giving orders and passing directives like old hands.

The kids were running the show now, and they knew it.

Countdown

As the frenetic pace increased, Glenn began to keep a diary on tape. The following chapters are paraphrased excerpts of the recordings he made during the summer of 1982.

Tuesday, August 17, 1982.

"For a long time now I've been anxious to get a tape recorder so that I could record some of the things that have been happening leading up to October first.

"I want to understand what we did, why we did it and perhaps the way we should have done it; because we're sure not doing it right. I'm convinced that for a long time to come there are going to be a lot of people looking at what we've done and saying we did it wrong. They're right – it should have been done a different way. We would like to have done it correctly, but we weren't given the time or resources. What we've done is the best we could with the resources and time we had.

"We've been working towards schedules from the beginning; schedules that don't mean anything because they're never kept – not even close. The original plans called for the design of American Adventure to be finished two years ago – and it isn't done yet.

"The schedule we're working toward today is to have the control system, all forty-some cabinets of it, functioning so that a show can be presented by September 13. The cabinets aren't even all in the building yet, so clearly that's not possible. But I do think that we'll make it by October 1st."

Midnight, Tuesday, August 17, 1982.

"I started at six o'clock this morning, eighteen hours ago.

"I need to make a schedule out for tomorrow that shows who's working what shifts. Most of us are putting in two shifts a day. We try to cover all the right shifts with the right people.

"My radio has gone out again."

6:00 AM, Wednesday, August 18, 1982

"Some of the mechanical engineers don't think we're working hard enough. I don't know where they're coming from. I know that they don't understand what we're doing, or what kind of problems we have. Last night we said we would have the system ready to run some time trials on the lifts, but we couldn't because some sensors were burned out. They just have to get used to the fact that sometimes things break down after successful runs."

4:30 PM, Wednesday, August 18, 1982

"I distributed a memo to my people today that says they're all on call 16 hours a day, 7 days a week. They took it pretty well. Our shifts are staggered the clock, but from 6:00 PM to 10:00 PM every night we're all in together. Unfortunately, on the weekends they schedule activities that require some of us to work over 24 hours consecutively.

"This morning we tried to do time trials on lift 9. Everyone was standing around with their stopwatches. We pushed the button and nothing happened, of course. It turned out that the construction workers had moved a wire so that they could raise the lift manually, and then reconnected it in the wrong spot. They've got no business doing that, it's asking for trouble."

3:42 AM, Thursday, August 19, 1982

"A major milestone: for the first time we successfully raised a lift from the animation console in the theater. That ought to build confidence. When you think about what we did, though, it seems kind of ridiculous. The animation console told a computer in Central to send a command to the monitor cabinet that distributes it to an animation cabinet that sends it to a ride control computer that sends it to a data concentrator that sends it through an RF cabinet that raises the lift. That seems like a lot of effort for something that we can do with a few switches."

3:40 PM, Saturday, August 21, 1982

"I had a meeting with Orlando Ferrante, John Zovich, Miller Andress, Norm Doerges, Jim Verity, Neil Gallagher, Cecil Robinson, Jane Jackson and Conrad. They wanted to know where American Adventure stood, particularly the electronics. After the presentation we looked pretty good. But the thing that struck me about the meeting was that this group of people has the ability to mobilize a lot of people and direct a lot of money and attention at a problem. Yet they don't really understand our systems. They'll take a little piece of information and go from there. As a result it's very important how that piece of information is worded. They're very intelligent people, but they don't understand today's electronic systems. It seems to me that they don't trust the managers who work for them.

"The coordinators are given a lot of access to the upper management; they assimilate information and pass it on to top management, completely bypassing the technical management in between. The trouble is that the coordinators are not qualified to interpret this information because they don't have the technical background, so they often come up with the wrong conclusions. It leaves me in the position of spending two thirds of my time fighting this sort of a thing rather than doing my job.

"In the course of troubleshooting several things in the pit today I get the feeling that everybody's hanging over our shoulders like vultures. They want to know what's going on, but every time we pass along a little bit of information they latch onto it and run around telling everybody, even if they don't understand it. If they would just leave us alone so we could do some serious troubleshooting, we could come up with some solutions. They're well intentioned, but counter-productive. We probably did a grand total of thirty minutes of troubleshooting spread out over an entire day of trying to explain to people what we were doing."

6:40 AM, Sunday, August 22, 1982

"Yesterday morning, my radio battery went dead for 2 hours while I was asleep. The phones are out at Fort Wilderness, so for 2 hours they couldn't find me. I've been catching hell all day long for not being available. Then this afternoon the radio completely went out. I guess I'll have to take it to radio repair again."

8:00 PM, Monday, August 23, 1982

"I fixed the radio with some parts out of another one that was broken, then I sent the broken one to radio repair. The ride programming computer was down, so Bob didn't get to do any programming today, but he worked on stage control hardware. The schedule in the pit has changed again. 6:00 AM to noon the contractors work on punchlist items, with the lifts stationary. Noon to midnight is spent animating the figures. Midnight to 6:00 AM is our stage control test-and-adjust. We've got meetings now at 6:30 AM, 11:00 AM, and 11:00 PM."

2:53 AM, Wednesday, August 25, 1982

"I'm going to skip the 6:00 AM meeting. It's a productive meeting, but it's been a long day. I think this is 21 hours."

6:00 PM, Wednesday, August 25, 1982

"I didn't come in until 1:00 PM today... Derek was in for 15 hours straight again. Bob worked a good 16 last night. Derek thinks we should all start to grow beards between now and opening. I'm not sure I can stand that.

"My radio went out again. I'm going to take it back to radio repair."

2:00 AM, Thursday, August 26, 1982

"My birthday. So that's a 13 hour day. Derek just came in for the last shift.

"I was thinking today how everybody's always looking for a leader. People don't seem to want to make decisions on their own. It makes it possible for a person who's willing to accept the responsibility to take charge and determine his own destiny.

"I've learned another valuable lesson, too. Never present your boss with your problems. Present him with your solutions. Allow him to think of you as a person who has problems to contend with, but always has solutions.

"Well so much for my wisdom for the day. Happy 25th birthday. A quarter of a century. I've got to hurry up and do some more living. I don't want to get to half a century and realize that there are a whole bunch of things I haven't done, and can't do because I don't have the health."

10:00 PM, Thursday, August 26, 1982

"My people got me lunch today. A pizza and a birthday cake over at the Sun Bank office. It was nice.

"I went to eat with Mom and Dad at the Howard Johnson's in Lake Buena Vista. I was late to meet them because a meeting ran over. It was another meeting with the vice-presidents and directors. It's funny, but I find that I have to present them with as little information as possible. It would be catastrophic if I were to tell them what all of our *real* problems are. They'd want to tell me how to solve them, and they have no idea. They don't really understand what we're doing. So I tell them about the problems we've solved. There are literally hundreds of problems that they never hear about.

"I have to worry about the real problems, like whether or not we're going to have monitor cabinet software. Now that's a real problem. I wonder if the other disciplines have this problem with management? Somehow I don't think to the same extent."

2:20 AM, Friday, August 27, 1982

"When I got to the building last night at 10:00 they had another birthday cake for me and they sang Happy Birthday over the PA system from the animation console in the theater. That was sure a surprise after the lunch and the cake at the Sun Bank today. Ed told a bunch of (department) 520 people today that he was very pleased with 510's performance. Coming from him that's a great compliment. I got the results of my blood tests back. They say that I'm OK. But I wish I had more energy and wasn't tired all the time. Derek finished the installation of electric eye break beams, another of our safety interlocks. It didn't work quite like we wanted.

To test it we placed a one-inch square of cardboard on top of the carriage and drove it forward so that the piece of cardboard passed through the break beam. Sure enough, when it broke the beam the drive motor turned off. But as the carriage slowed down it coasted right through the piece of cardboard and then the drive motor started up again. We're going to have to make it latch.

Interlocks are supposed to be simple. But now we've got another level of complexity going in. The more levels deep we go, the more opportunities there are for somebody to put in a jumper to override the interlocks. The reality of the matter is that people put in jumpers. And then they forget to take the jumpers off. We've already seen it happen. Fortunately it hasn't cost us anything. There's always been an interlock or bumper to back up the one that was defeated. But we've come close.

"Safety guidelines such as not working under an active lift are readily violated. You wouldn't catch me under there for anything. I don't know how safe the system is, and I designed it. They have such great faith in one lousy switch or valve. But when I catch them doing it and tell them that it's not safe, their general foreman says that he wishes I wouldn't tell his people that what they're doing is unsafe."

7:00 PM, Friday, August 27, 1982

"It looks like we're real close to being able to have Francie substitute for Bob. She's going to take part of Bob's work tomorrow between 8:00 AM and noon. I'm going to try to keep Bob's hours today down to about 12 so that he can go for a 16 or 18 tomorrow. But I know that he's not getting more than 6 hours of sleep a night because he's only away from the building about 8 hours a day."

2:55 AM, Saturday, August 28, 1982

"I'm driving from Fort Wilderness to the Site. I see that Bob's not back to his trailer, so he must be out at American Adventure doing testing with Ed. He'd better get out of there soon, because he's got to be back in before noon.

"A lot of this place is lit up at night, now. They don't shut off Spaceship Earth's lights until after 2:00 AM now. It's a pretty impressive view, looking at it through the steel work for Horizons just as I come in past the guard shack."

3:00 PM, Saturday, August 28, 1982

"Production Services in California called and said they had all the parts to build a cabinet that we released, but that they needed a few questions answered. We just replied, 'It's OK, we've already built it. It's been in the building and functioning for three months.'

"Every single thing we've released to Production Services has been delayed, sometimes lost. The only way it's ever recovered is if we personally take charge of it to get it out of the bogged down mire of paperwork and confusion. Fortunately two thirds of what we've released we've just built ourselves. We never even let them know what was happening.

"Animation programming has sure had a lot of setbacks, including Central problems, animation cabinet problems, stage control problems, figure problems, projection problems, hydraulic problems, mechanical problems. They've been delayed to the point where Jane has decided that animation programming is going to go to 16 hours a day. In a couple of weeks it will go to 24. So now Bob and Francie will have to support the stage control system 24 hours a day.

"Last night Bob made a real salient comment. He said that the animation programmers ought to look over the proscenium wall once in awhile. It's true. They forget how complex the system is. They need to develop some patience with the things they find so frustrating.

"It's essential that people communicate to increase the efficiency of the operation, but I'm not sure to what extent the efficiency can be increased when you're fighting lack of sleep and frustration. Days seem so short that we can't piece together enough of them. There's no concept of when they begin and end, or what day it is, unless you look at the calendar or your watch.

"About 4:00 PM today we had a big thunderstorm and a lot of rain. Weather reporting from Control is pretty good. When they say it's going to rain it usually does. If it's going to be a bad rainstorm they declare a 10-100 (emergency traffic only) on the radio. Most of the Future World pavilions called in power losses, including emergency power losses. Apparently American Adventure wasn't affected."

2:30 PM, Sunday, August 29, 1982

"At the 11:30 meeting they agreed to give us a couple of days without having to support figure programming so that we can work out the bugs in our stage control system.

"We never got the test and adjust time to work out all the small problems. We got to the point where the system was barely functional and immediately they took control of it. The schedule is so compressed that now we're going through simultaneous programming and test and adjust.

"They're going to bring in two animation consoles so that they won't waste so much time switching from one part of the show to another.

"Ed wants to make a couple of changes to the hydraulics. The reprogramming effort involved is going to eat up a portion of the time we just got to work out our problems. But it will fix several things, including the fact that the 'fast down' valves don't make the lifts go down faster. Anyway, Ed says that he doesn't need the 'fast down' valve again. He had originally thought he did, then thought he didn't, then thought he did, and now he thinks he doesn't. It's not something we can be critical of, though; it's evolution."

3:30 PM, Sunday, August 29, 1982

"I need to remember to get some sort of power line filter for all seven of the processor cabinets in the pavilion, because we have so many electrical failures due to the weather. When the lightning comes, we very often lose data. The uninterruptible power supplies don't seem to filter the line very well. Most of the time they aren't even uninterruptible."

2:00 AM, Monday, August 30, 1982

"My two biggest problems are sleep and food.

"I could exist with this little sleep if it was at least on a regular basis, but it's so irregular. I try to listen for my call sign on the radio when I'm asleep. This morning I was awakened by the radio after about four hours of sleep. Then I couldn't get back to sleep because I'd had four hours.

"The trouble with food is that when you're sleepy and hungry, sleep wins out, so I seem to be missing a lot of meals. But when I eat, I eat big meals. My timing is completely messed up, eating at all the wrong times. I haven't bothered to put food in the refrigerator since I moved into the trailer in February because the schedule is so erratic that anything I buy just seems to spoil. I just eat out. All the food begins to taste the same, since it all comes from the same place here on the property. It's been two weeks since I've been off the property.

"I've been regularly turning in an average of 100 hours a week. My folks ask, 'How can they expect you to work these hours?' It's not 'they,' that's just what it takes to get the job done. I have a commitment to get the job done. I'm not forcing the folks who work for me to put in these hours. They're working these hours because they started something and they have to finish it. It takes this amount of time to get it done. Every time you don't sleep with the radio on, or don't make yourself available regardless of the time, you find yourself spending two days trying to get yourself out of some mess that you could have resolved in a few minutes, had you been available.

"The managers say we have to get away from it, we have to get some sleep, but the same people are saying, 'I don't care what it takes, get this done, get that done.' Of course they're doing the same thing themselves."

5:40 AM, Monday, August 30, 1982

"Just got out of the building after looking at the cabinet that drives the small carriage. It sure is messed up. They haven't given me any assurance that the motor is under warranty since the flood."

6:30 PM, Monday, August 30, 1982

"We had some unknown people prowling around our monitor cabinet. It turned out that they were asked by Brian to do some tests on it. Their approach was to take all the cables off the back, which makes figure programming kind of difficult."

7:49 PM, Tuesday, August 31, 1982

"It's been an interesting day in the life of American Adventure. Out at the building we were confronted with two problems, both very significant.

"First, we discovered that the carriage was not able to make its moves in the prescribed amount of time. The reason is not a limitation in the drive motor, but because we can't get the lifts down fast enough to allow time to move the carriage before the next lift has to be raised, since the interlocks won't let the carriage move with any lifts up. Bob's proposed solution involves enabling the carriage to move before the lift is down. But that eliminates one line of defense. Ed's proposed solution is to increase the downward speed of the lifts by putting weight on them or utilizing the 'fast down' valve.

Second, it was pointed out by the animation people that the actuator that raises the raft severely jolts the figure when it stops. The only way to solve that problem is to use a variable speed drive system. I called Doug Gingrich at Reliance Electric, and he came out with John Nacy. As usual, the bottom line is not going to be expense. It's going to be lead-time: How fast can we implement the solution?"

11:22 AM, Wednesday, September 1, 1982

"I suppose I'm guilty of not running to Melanie, our coordinator, and telling her about the problem with the carriage moves not being fast enough. But before we can tell them what needs to be done, there's no sense in alarming them, because all we'll get is a whole bunch of advice about how to fix the problem."

10:21 PM, Wednesday, September 1, 1982

"Just met Steve at the stoplight to give him replacements for two sensors that failed. He's identified a new problem. We forgot to run power to the liquid nitrogen controller. He threw an extension cord out to it."

12:39 AM, Thursday, September 2, 1982

"I spent some time yesterday going over the list of things to be completed with Melanie. We really haven't completed very many things on the list. When we go in front of the vice-presidents and directors it makes it look like we haven't accomplished anything. The only explanation I can think of is that we're spending so much time solving unanticipated problems.

"We're beginning to throw out more and more things that we'd wanted for Opening Day. Realistically, I'm at the point where I'm going to have to throw out the Emergency-stop buttons. At one point I thought we could get those in, but now there's not a chance."

3:26 AM, Thursday, September 2, 1982

"Until we get the automatic controls, to move the Statue of Liberty torch and balcony set up we have to violate the interlock, open the door, turn the door interlock breaker, and then run the controls from inside the high voltage section. In the course of bringing the torch up I observed three problems. One, when you push the up button on the balcony it starts up, stops, and then after about 5 seconds it starts again and goes all the way to the top. Two, when it gets to the top the motor keeps humming. Three, it won't come back down."

4:24 PM, Thursday, September 2, 1982

"They're upset that the large carriage monitor cabinet doesn't work. Nobody seems to remember that they never gave us a chance to check it out.

"They just had an animation oil leak. The fluid level sensor that I had Frank put in the other day saved them from a bigger oil spill. It's kind of nice to see something work."

7:39 AM, Friday, September 3, 1982

"The curtain controls were completely miswired at the connectors in one of the animation cabinets. You could tell that it had been undone and redone. Somebody must have thought that they were doing us a favor, but they completely messed it up. Everything went nuts, and Derek had to go running to the equipment room and hit all the E-Stops. That took a good hour to straighten out."

12:07 PM, Friday, September 3, 1982

"I got my other radio back from radio repair. Sure enough, it stopped working in less than an hour again.

"Conrad had a meeting at 10:00 AM to tell us that Lee Frisius, our section head in California, turned in his resignation effective October 1. No replacement was announced."

10:12 AM, Saturday, September 4, 1982

"I got a call from Evelyn to tell me about a meeting to discuss the activities on Labor Day. Since we aren't participating I suggested that it wasn't really important for me to attend.

"I got a call from Bob, reporting that the payload down sensors had not been wired in. He found this out because he accidentally issued a command and the carriage started moving toward the rear projection screen while a lift was still coming down. Apparently it just barely cleared, and scared them all to death."

Noon, Saturday, September 4, 1982

"I tell you, having a full night's sleep and a full stomach sure gives you a different outlook on life.

11:25 PM, Saturday, September 4, 1982

"Brian had the bright idea of having one of the maintenance guys take care of some simple wiring additions. That's the way it should be done. We're spending too much time fixing things ourselves. We identified 24 wires that had to be crimped and installed. It took him more than four hours. I couldn't believe it. I swear I could have had it done in 45 minutes.

"Today Rick was pushing us for the 'Intolerable Acts' scrim, one of the pieces of rigging that's lowered during the show. Derek said 'Well, I haven't had a chance to check it out yet, but we can go ahead and try it.' So he issued the command and down it came. That was OK, except they didn't want to take it all the way down. Rick called him on the radio and said 'Stop it! Stop it!' Derek flipped the switches off, but then realized that it was a latching curtain controller, and there was no way to stop it. Rick called back and said 'Stop it before it hits the cherry picker!' So Derek went running for the winch room, where he realized that there were 17 curtain controllers on the wall, and he didn't know which E-stop to hit. So he started hitting all the E-stops as fast as he could, and finally stopped it after it had already hit the cherry picker. Fortunately it didn't hurt anything, but it could have if it had gone any further. It was another case of being pushed to do things too fast."

"Back in February we had meeting in which it was decided that we'd have two weeks to check out this cabinet, and two weeks for that one, and all those two week periods wouldn't overlap. It was a beautiful plan, although it seemed so tight that we could just barely get by. All of those check out periods vanished. Now they say 'Is the cabinet installed? Might it work? OK, let's use it.' Then, of course, we turn it on and it doesn't work and people are annoyed."

6:22 PM, Sunday, September 5, 1982

"The uninterruptible power supplies are worthless. Out of five, four didn't survive a two-second power glitch during the storm today."

12:02 AM, Monday, September 6, 1982

"I spent the evening crawling through the carriage checking out animation cabinets with an oscilloscope. While trying to get to the one under set three that's mounted sideways I dropped the scope down through 14 feet of steel jungle. It landed on the concrete floor. Amazingly, it came up working. Let's hear it for Tektronix.

Later, Derek did a high-speed crash test on the large carriage. He placed a three-inch-wide piece of cardboard on top of it and ran it at full speed toward the projection screen. It stopped one foot before the screen, due to the break beams. That was a big relief.

"I overheard Mark today when he didn't know I was listening. I was checking some interlocks and he said 'Glenn is just a young engineer who doesn't want to see his first design self-destruct in his face, so he puts interlocks on everything.' I suppose that's not too far from the truth.

"The radio is alive tonight with people getting ready for the Construction Family Labor Day Preview Opening this morning. Norm Doerges, Jim Nagy and Cecil Robinson are all on the radio worrying about every little thing. All the coordinators, all the project managers. It's the first time I've seen Jane here at this hour of the night ever, and American Adventure doesn't even run tomorrow."

8:30 AM, Monday, September 6, 1982

"It seems they had bad luck last night. They can't get the carriage to move the required distance and get the lifts down and back up in the allotted time. Bob, Mark and Ed wound up staying all night. Bob still thinks they can do it if they can just issue the commands fast enough. They've got to shave off 12 seconds. It seems like it's going to be mighty tight. Mark and Ed think we're going to have to make some concessions and move the carriage while the lifts are still falling."

11:28 AM, Monday, September 6, 1982

"Well, EPCOT Center is open, sort of. It sure is strange to see guests in the theater. Of course the show isn't there, but they're watching the figures being programmed.

"Energy's been having a real hard time staying up. But apparently the other shows are doing pretty well."

8:00 PM, Monday, September 6, 1982

"It's been kind of a fun day. I've been wandering around, seeing what there was to see. An amazing transformation has taken place in the last few days. It was a real shock to see people walking through the park. Somehow I feel that now I have to share something that was all mine."

Labor Day

The Great Scimitar of opening day took an unexpected swing in mid-summer of 1982. The company announced that there was to be a special preview, a trial run, on Labor Day, September 6. Although the preview was for Construction Workers, not the general public, the word was that everything must work.

A general sense of shock pervaded the construction site. "Labor Day? You must be joking, it's a month early!" It was almost as if everyone had expected to finish the whole thing on September 29th, go home and sleep for a day, then open it on October first without testing it.

Labor Day was never a more accurate term for the first Monday in September. So close to opening day that to call it short notice is a case of remarkable exaggeration, management decided that EPCOT was not going to open October 1 as planned. Instead, there would be a special construction worker preview on September 6. Labor Day had the most impact on Linda and Chris Senchack because they had the most pavilions, and of course, the Retreat gang, who in a manner of speaking had ALL the pavilions.

Strangely enough, many of the engineers seemed to function better, as the cutting edge of the Scimitar grew closer. The scramble brought a new facet to department 510: stardom. Everybody, at least on the front lines, was a star for about five or six days. If your project was really hot, every executive on the site knew your name. And when you signed in on the radio in the morning, everybody but God started talking to you (and He was standing in line).

Of course, in the confusion, some massive mistakes were barely averted.

For example, at one point shortly before opening, an engineer and a tech decided that the wirelists were all backwards, that the positive and negative voltages listed did not correspond to actual plus and minus. This was because neither of them were in California for a big meeting when the department discussed unusual notation used in the lists. David had been sitting in the meeting, as a wirelister, understanding absolutely none of the technical jargon that was going on, but for some reason it stuck in his mind.

He recalls:

"It was late in September. The engineer and tech said, 'All the wirelists are backwards, all the monitor cabinets are backwards, what are we going to do?' I said, 'Well, look, let's talk to California, let's not go crazy, let's find out what's wrong and what we can do to correct it, and go through the proper channels.' They said, 'No, no, it's too late. We can't do that; if we go back to California now it will be a panic. What we have to do is get a couple of techs out there and rewire all the cabinets before anybody finds out,' I said, 'No, you're wrong. Here is what happened, I was at the meeting when they explained it, let me explain it to you.'"

"So as a complete layperson I sat down and tried to explain to them why the cabinets were correct. But they kept asking, 'Well, how come it doesn't do this, how come it doesn't do that?' I couldn't reason with them as an engineer; all I could do was repeat by rote what I had heard at the meeting. They said, 'You don't know anything about electronics, so shut up, we're right, you shouldn't even be involved with this.'"

"Finally, I convinced them to pose a hypothetical question to Chris, since he was at the meeting. At first they argued, 'No, no, Chris is too smart, he'll figure out what's going on and he'll tell everybody that the cabinets are backwards.' But at last I convinced them. The engineer went to Chris and asked, 'Chris, if the cabinets were wired and signal and return meant plus and minus would the cabinets work?' Chris said, 'Of course not.' The engineer looked at him and asked, 'Why not?' Chris explained everything to him exactly as I had explained it the night before, but with some key engineering points that I hadn't known."

"The engineer just looked at me and said, 'Oh, oh okay, great.' Later, he told the tech. But neither of them ever said a single word to me. They never said, 'You were right,' they never said, 'I'm sorry we called you an idiot,' they never said a word. That was the end of the subject. I guess we were all a little crazy at that point."

* * *

David's experience illustrates what was at times really scary about EPCOT. With all of the autonomy, anything not being destroyed by chance was so much a matter of coincidence. As in the example, if the right person hadn't been in the right place at the proverbial right time, a potentially disastrous engineering decision would have been made.

Another example of serendipity was when Steve, near the end of August, suddenly realized that American Adventure could absolutely not run without its monitor cabinet because the entire show cycle – starting the show, controlling the doors and houselights – all depended on the monitor cabinet. There was no way to run it manually. It was an impossibility. Steve recalls:

"When I suddenly realized this, I just dropped everything. I left the pavilion where Glenn was having problems with buffer expander cards. I left Bob Frye still debugging the ride control system, but knowing that the hardware was now working. And I sat down for a solid month to program the monitor cabinet. I wrote my own real time operating system from scratch. It was finally ready to try about September 25th, and we were able to cycle a show in a rudimentary fashion."

* * *

But in the midst of the confusion there arose heroics.

The China pavilion had been the bastard from early in EPCOT's construction. It seemed that nobody took it seriously in the scheme of things. It was the last pavilion to be done. It was classified as a minor pavilion, meaning that it didn't have any animation in it and nobody worried about it too much. Linda had done the design for the show control system and the monitor system for the China pavilion in two weeks in California prior to when she left for Florida. That was unheard of.

Little construction work had been done on it. Then it was announced that it too, would open on Labor Day.

Linda remembers that when she heard about the Labor Day pre-opening, "I walked over to the China pavilion. I knew that they intended that it be open. At that time there were no projectors in it, there were no screens up, and the building was just a shell. There was no equipment in it whatsoever. Only temporary power. I had the Transportation Pavilion, the France Pavilion, the Canada Pavilion all to worry about, and I figured "Well, China, they're just not going to make it, I'm not even going to think about it." Son of a gun, about 10 days before Labor Day they came to me and they asked what cables were required to open the show, so I went to the cable schedule with the electrical contractor and I checked them off. I said, "Well, if you get these pulled they'll be able to run a show. This is the minimum configuration I need to do it." The electronic equipment was wheeled into place. In less than a week we presented our first show. It had been connected, powered, and tested in a matter of days. That was a surprise for everybody."

After some more hundred-hour weeks and 36- and 48-hour sleepless shifts, the Labor Day preview came off, perhaps not perfectly, but far better than some had feared, and euphoria ran high. For example, China's queue area was boarded up with plywood, the cement floor was filthy, there was no carpeting, and some of the areas were cordoned off. There was no place to sit at that point. They just herded everybody in. In terms of the normal Disney concern for aesthetics, it was crazy. The main reason China opened on Labor Day was because they realized they needed all the attractions they could get to handle the crowd. They opened it because it could process 3,000 people an hour. Essentially, it was like showing it in a warehouse with nine screens.

Surprisingly, China ran flawlessly all Labor Day. Everyone who knew the background story was stunned. To this day, not even Linda knows how it happened.

Most of the ex-Cals were very impressed on Labor Day. It was their first opportunity to see a lot of those shows. Most people, particularly those who were not in engineering, could take off an hour or two to go around to see the shows.

Not all the ex-Cals had the luxury of seeing the sights. Jamie, Linda and Brian spent all day nursing their pavilions and didn't dare leave.

Linda sat in the projection room at China all day and Jamie took Canada and France. They finally got the guts to leave about 6:00 o'clock in the evening. They took a real quick walk around what the site for about 10 minutes. They couldn't have done it without the radios, which kept them from being out of touch with PICO base.

David recalls:

"I felt a tremendous sense of guilt that day because there was a lot to be done and I took off four hours to walk around. I went around by myself through all the pavilions and saw what I could. At one point, I passed by Jamie rushing by with his radio in hand and I felt really guilty. I thought, 'I'm taking off this time, and he is working his butt off.'

"The day was almost ruined for me by something that happened when I saw the Harvest Theater show in the Land Pavilion. I was impressed with the entire show, almost to the point of tears. It was so well done. After the show, I was walking out with all the construction workers and their families and I heard one guy say to another, 'Well, what did you think of the film?' The other one said, 'Like near put me to sleep.' The first guy said, 'Yeah, it was awful.' I remember wanting to go up and throttle them both, I was so offended. Knowing Chris and all the work he put into that, all the work all of us put into it, and hearing these two construction workers slough it off as if it were meaningless."

* * *

Despite the overall favorable impression of the engineers, there was still an impending shadow of the Scimitar cutting across the landscape. Pretending to have an opening day showed just how much had to be done to arrive at the real thing.

The most obvious illustration of how much was left to be done, was the state of the entire CommuniCore area just a week before Labor Day. It was still completely dirt except they had poured the cement for the planters. There was no planting or even cement to walk on in the entire area. You couldn't even see from pavilion to pavilion because of the mounds of dirt. One side of CommuniCore had no glass in it.

But on Labor Day, most of us finally began to believe that the park would open on October 1st. If one walked around and saw things working and heard the next day's downtime report (which was remarkably good), one would realize that there could be a functioning park that the public could enjoy on October 1st.

A few engineers had a mini-party in Brian's trailer the night of the Labor Day victory. Linda and Steve and David and Ron Bittner and Jamie and Brian and Andrew were there. It was a manic/depressive hour or two of sipping wine, telling stories of success and failure, and expressing fears and hopes, mixed with the sudden realization: "My God, there's not even a month left. How will I do everything I have to in that amount of time?" Nobody got drunk and ran through the campground naked singing, "Zip-a-Dee-Doo-Dah."

David recalls:

"That night, even more than October 1st, was the culmination of everything that we'd been working on so hard for years. There we were, a bunch of youngsters, and we had just pulled off the most incredible coup of our lives, but nobody had the energy to get up and dance. We were all just sort of sprawled around the room. I think that was because everyone was not only exhausted from the effort to get there, but also intimidated at the month ahead.

"Most of us took the next day off. That was the first day that some of the engineers had had off in months."

****

The only sign of nervousness was expressed in the fear, "Is there life after EPCOT?" It was not the first time the great shakeout fear had been expressed, since the company had called a series of meetings in the early summer to reveal its "Consolidation Plan." Consolidation of the Company's size by... who knew how much?

Management claimed that through the magic of Consolidation, not one person would be laid off or fired. The term became a long-running, though not very funny, joke. (Job applicant to prospective employer: "Well sir, I never really left my last job, I was Consolidated. I just stopped getting a paycheck. I guess I'm still a Disney employee.") And perhaps they always would be.

But there was not much time to consider the thoughts expressed that night. The Great Scimitar continued its slow, sweeping descent, removing calendar pages and slices of sanity with each arc. The big slice was yet to come. October 1 was less than four weeks away.

The Eleventh Hour

Glenn's tapes reveal more insight as opening day neared:

Midnight, Monday, September 6, 1982

"It's been an interesting time since 8:00 PM. Bob came in to try some code he wrote early this morning to compress the lift times. It was a series of one error after another. We issued the command and didn't see anything. It turned out someone had unplugged the cable to look for a data problem. Next the lift wouldn't go all the way up. Then we couldn't get it down. Bob thought it looked like low pressure. Sure enough, we sent Dan back into the tunnel, and he found that the pump had a bad pressure switch. Finally we got enough pressure to the system to bring the lift up in time. Then we couldn't find anyone at central to sign the animation console back on. Finally we ran it, but it was still two seconds too slow. Watching set 2 come down we discovered that we could actually issue the carriage command two seconds earlier. The bottom line is that it can be done, Bob was right. The time was well spent."

9:34 AM, Tuesday, September 7, 1982

"We need to instruct the maintenance people on how to trouble-shoot the animation cards. There are a lot of test points and indicator lights on those cards, which they're not using properly because they don't know what they mean."

Noon, Tuesday, September 7, 1982

"I spent the morning in the electronic engineering office. I ran into John Zovich and Miller Andress. Everyone was very concerned because they had talked to Jane Jackson. She was depressed because we hadn't been able to make the carriage and lift moves in the prescribed amount of time, and it didn't look like we were going to be able to. Fortunately, last night we had resolved all of those problems and made it work. I passed the good news along to John and Miller."

12:20 AM, Wednesday, September 8, 1982

"They want to open the park to employees on the 24th. That means we've got 2 weeks until we need a complete show. We're supposed to run a show for the president, Dick Nunis, on Friday, and another one for the executive committee on Monday or Tuesday. Right now we haven't run anything even close to a full show and we've got just three days left. It's really scary. We could blow it very easily at this point. There are so many things that could get us.

"Jane and Rick and I decided that it doesn't make sense to write schedules anymore. Everything that's going on in the pit is too compressed. The biggest problem is not having the particular person who is needed at a given moment. Too much time is wasted waiting for people who are sleeping their six hours. It's become impossible to stick to a schedule beyond a few hours – things change so fast. The new plan is to have everybody in the pit from 8:00 AM until midnight. Then we can get our sleep between midnight and 8:00 AM. Animation programming will proceed 24 hours a day. The most difficult thing will be enforcing the midnight quitting time. If we're into something we're not going to want to leave. Take tonight. Guys are still out there. People are talking about sleeping in the VIP lounge to save the five-mile drive to Fort Wilderness."

1:34 PM, Wednesday, September 8, 1982

"I did some paperwork describing what the lights mean on the circuit boards and passed it out to all the maintenance folks. They

133

seemed to receive it well, but I think it may be a case of telling the plumber all about your electrical problems."

7:11 PM, Wednesday, September 8, 1982

"I'm going to escape for a meal and run up to Apopka for the last time for a while. In the pit, Bob just cycled the large carriage through an entire 'show' from the programmer's console. The programmers put in all the times on the tape and played the whole thing back from start to finish. Every lift managed to come up in time including every carriage move. It was very encouraging. I talked to Bob about making some modifications in the program so that if a lift does not make it up in time, rather than hanging up the computer just lowers it and raises the next one. That way we won't lose an entire show."

2:08 PM, Thursday, September 9, 1982

"We found a strange thing in one of the animation cabinets. Somebody had moved the cables to the wrong connectors. There's no good explanation. It must have been sabotage."

6:08 PM, Thursday, September 9, 1982

"Charlie is up in arms because Walt and Steve and Frank have been rewiring cabinets without them being advised. Now they're locking up the animation cards so that we can't get to them. It's almost as bad as the union situation before the construction labor got out. Unfortunately, Steve and Walt have a tendency to do it in whatever is the fastest way. Locking up cards in an attempt to keep us from fixing cabinets is a pretty silly attitude. For three years we designed this attraction. Now they're telling us they don't think we're competent to fix it."

12:44 AM, Friday, September 10, 1982

"The day is finally over. Finally, this evening we got all the data coming to the pavilion straightened out. We had a lightning storm today that knocked out four out of five cabinets that have uninterruptible power supplies. Steve dropped by. He's made some progress on monitor cabinet software. He's got a display running. We have to have that to open."

10:45 PM, Friday, September 10th, 1982

"Today was the big day that the show was supposed to run for Dick Nunis. Just as we might have figured, it didn't come about. Strangely enough, it was not because of electronics or hydraulics or any of the customary problems, but because when they finally tried to put all of the show data into the computer at Central at once, it wouldn't fit! They're working on the problem now in Central. I guess it's an indication how much bigger a show American Adventure is than anything else.

"After all the precautions and interlocks, today we raised a lift into the cherry picker. It could have been much, much worse than it was, but we just barely snagged the corner. It broke one of the little spires off the Centennial set. If it had been positioned slightly differently it would have completely wiped out the lift. We were very lucky.

"This morning very early we were working on the animation cabinets when we happened across a cut power cord. Obviously sabotage. It was nice that it was a power cord because those are easy to identify. A signal line somewhere would have been much more difficult.

"All the curtains are working now. We haven't really run them from the show control system, but they're all verified, and I don't expect any trouble."

10:19 AM, Saturday, September 11, 1982

"Last night they ran a show and none of the curtains worked."

7:46 PM, Saturday, September 11th, 1982

"Walt and I worked on curtains all day. Bob and Ed had a problem raising set 11. Naturally we had no documentation, but it appeared that the command was not getting there. I called Steve at the bank and he drew a mental picture for us over the phone. It took us a while to figure out because it was not the sort of a problem we were expecting. A wire was connected to the wrong spot. The funny thing is that 20 minutes earlier it had been working fine. There's no way it could have worked that way. Somebody moved the wire, but I don't know how they could and not be caught in that amount of time. Anyway, I straightened it out and it's been working fine since. The flying sailor wouldn't go up. Although the Reliance guy left it in working condition, apparently something's gone wrong. I stumbled across an incredible amount of garbage today, things that should be corrected later on. For example, I found wires twisted together in a junction box from a time months ago when I made a lift work. It was never fixed properly."

1:12 AM, Sunday, September 12, 1982

"We isolated two more problems. It took a long time to find them because everybody knows for a fact that they'd been fine. So who changed them? We also found two bad power supplies, and there are no more spares."

1:30 AM, Monday, September 13, 1982

"Bob and Ed came in at 2:00 PM to run a show with lifts only, no animation. The first attempt ran fairly well until two of the lifts failed to come up. We tried another show and again didn't get all the way through. On the third and fourth tries we did, and everyone was fairly pleased.

"While we were working, the strangest thing happened. One of the traveler curtains started moving. Then pretty soon another one, and then the main contour curtain. They started cycling up and down for no apparent reason. I looked at the animation cabinet, and it appeared to be getting a random spray of data from Central. I shut off all the commands, but the curtains kept running because the curtain control cabinets latch the data. So then I made a mad dash to the winch room and shut off all the breakers. It was all kind of exciting. It turned out the problem was caused by cables at Central.

That sure points out a vulnerable spot, since we messed up some of the rigging on the curtains."

12:38 PM, Monday, September 13, 1982

"They wanted the houselights up, so Rick called Jane on the radio and said, 'Turn up the houselights.' Jane responded, 'I'm trying, I'm trying.' I don't know where she was, but she wasn't anywhere near the houselight controls. I was. She kept saying, 'Has this got it? Has this got it?' I walked over and flipped the switch on and Rick radioed 'Thank you, Jane. We've got the houselights now.' I'm sure Jane thought she'd turned the houselights on!"

8:00 PM, Monday, September 13, 1982

"Steve called on the radio and asked if he could come out between shows to work on some of the output points from the monitor cabinet. I said 'Sure, between shows you should be able to slip in some time.' Wathel Rogers broke in on the radio and said, 'No, under no circumstances will anybody touch the monitor cabinet.' He's very concerned that something will go wrong before the executive committee showing tomorrow.

"I've got two points. One, the executive committee isn't supposed to postpone our work. Two, working on monitor cabinet software has absolutely no affect on the operation of the portion of the cabinet we need for the executive committee showing. It's completely harmless. I don't know who could know that better than the people who designed it.

"By this time a lot of important people had gathered in the theater to watch. We tried to run a show with both lifts and animation. But as set 2 started to come up there was a horrible grinding sound. Everybody went running to the proscenium wall."

12:53 AM, Tuesday, September 14, 1982

"We're still trying to get the show together for the 10:00 AM arrival of the executive committee, but it seems that the more time we put in, the farther we get from it. The grinding sound was one of the I-beams on lift 2 bending. We don't know why it happened or how serious it is yet. They're cutting it with a torch."

4:00 AM, Tuesday, September 14, 1982 [sounds unconscious]

"The whole problem seems to be hydraulic pressure, or lack of it. I think that we're all about asleep. I fell asleep for a little while underneath set 9. I'm going to get a blanket [yawn] and go back in."

1:04 PM, Tuesday, September 14, 1982

"Finally back on the road. First time since I parked the car at the building at 10:00 AM yesterday morning. It turned out that they found too much hydraulic pressure. As a result, lift 2 went up and bent the I-beam.

"I had just settled in for a forty minute nap under set 9 when I got the news. I was trying to snuggle up to the monitor cabinet with a blanket for another twenty minutes when they asked me to measure the voltage to a solenoid. I figured I'd go out there, see my 24 volts and go back to sleep. But it was 14 volts. I was amazed. I checked another one, and it was the same way. I went back to the control cabinet and found that it was working fine, shipping 24 volts out. I wondered where the other 10 volts was going. I found it across the lift enable switch, an interlock to prevent the lift from going up underneath the rear projection screen. I went to one of the switches to find out if it was faulty. When I took the cover off I found small gauge wire in it. That was an obvious explanation. It seems that in our word of mouth communications to the BVCC construction people we didn't get across the point that it needed to be heavier wire. I checked the other lifts and found that they all had the same problem. Apparently it had been barely enough in the past to work, but it was not sufficient to do the job properly. In fact it explained a lot of the problems that Ed had been attributing to mechanics or hydraulics.

"It's a very long line, and extremely difficult to replace because of where it is under the carriage, so in order to get us running I jumpered out all of the lift enable switches. That was something I had forbidden BVCC from ever doing, and I didn't want to do myself because of the risk to any set piece that might come up under the rear projection screen, but I didn't have much choice at the moment.

"The bent I-beam was not significant enough to stop us from using the lifts. They just had to readjust the chains to make up for the damage.

"By now it was 7:00 AM and the executive committee, was scheduled to be there at 10:00 AM. The immediate question was, 'Do we or do we not run the show without the interlocks?' By removing them, we had removed the second line of defense. The third line of defense was to have been the pressure sensors that we'd never installed. And the first line of defense was to have been the software check that Bob hadn't had time to implement yet. Without those three sets of interlocks the stage control system will execute any command that the show control system issues. But because of the data problems, as evidenced by the curtains the other day, the show control system can't be relied upon. But they wanted very badly to run this show because the executive committee is so worried; they've seen all the other shows run, but not ours. We've never been ready. On one hand I felt I should declare that it was unsafe. I could have held them to that. But I also felt that if we positioned people to keep an eye on things we could get through it. I pointed out that the people who would be keeping an eye on things had been awake for 24 hours. I also pointed out that I was making a decision without any sleep and that common sense and more sleep would probably tell me not to let it run at all.

"By 7:30 AM the news had spread. Orlando Ferrante and Jack Taylor were in the pit asking questions. Pretty soon it was Norm Doerges and John Zovich. They were all willing to let me make the decision.

"So we geared up to do it. By now it was 9:30 AM. Conrad came by and I discussed it with him. He was very displeased. He thought that I should put my foot down. He said it was a case of doing something unsafe and non-productive for a 'dog and pony show.' He believed that it was inappropriate. I believe that it was very Disney.

"Pretty soon Steve came in. After he'd been there about 15 minutes in the dark I mentioned to him that I'd just disabled all his lift enables. He was overcome with amazement. He couldn't believe that I was allowing this to happen.

"We put everybody in their positions, cleared the simplex frequency for American Adventure traffic, and waited about 15 minutes.

"The executive committee arrived. We ran the show.

The first lift came up, went down. The second lift came up, went down. The carriage then made its most difficult move. Set 3 came up. But it didn't go down.

"It never made it quite to the top, and the computer was waiting for that before it would process the down command. We hadn't had time to put in the software change that would have saved it. We tried to fool it by tripping the up sensors by hand, but one was too difficult to reach safely. The show animation, projection, audio and lighting continued with that set in the wrong position, but the carriage wouldn't move with the lift up. We started lowering it manually. By now the show had progressed past sets 4, 5 and 6, and was approaching the 7th. Of course the sets hadn't gone up, so although the animation was progressing, it wasn't visible from the audience, because the figures were down in the carriage.

"With set 3 finally down, we were contemplating whether we could do anything to get caught up with the show, when set seven's roof went up, because it was an animation function. This instantly reminded me that shortly the depression set roof and Teddy Roosevelt were going to go up due to animation commands. But they were still in the tunnel under the audience, where there was no place for them to go. The show could only be stopped from the animation console in the audience, so I radioed up to Rick, that he should stop the show immediately to prevent any damage. Teddy Roosevelt was on set 8, and we were already on set 7. There was no response on the radio. I repeated the message, but no one was listening or they couldn't hear over the audio. I grabbed Bob's headset and got Davie at the animator's console, just as Teddy Roosevelt stood up. The show stopped.

"The executive committee walked out. Ron Miller made the comment, 'We ought to let these people get back to work. They obviously have plenty to do.'

"I don't know what the perception was, but it definitely wasn't good.

"Shortly thereafter we got the carriage out from under the audience. Teddy had knocked his hat off, dirtied his jacket, and rubbed a hole in the ceiling insulation, but he didn't appear to be harmed.

"The carriage is stationary now for a lot of work that has to be done, including rewiring the lift enable switches so that we won't have to go through this idiocy again. Steve and I designed some interlocks to prevent animation commands from taking place underneath the audience. There's a lot to be done. We never did find out why lift 3 didn't make it all the way to the top."

8:53 PM, Tuesday, September 14, 1982

"Steve says they made good progress today. The lift enable switches are already all wired in. He's had good luck bringing up the monitor cabinet. I'm going to get a bite to eat before I go in."

5:04 AM, Thursday, September 16, 1982

"I came in yesterday at 10:00 AM, so this has been 19 hours. We had a 1:00 PM meeting with Bongiorno, Nagy, Ferrante, Zovich, Wathel, Jane, Ed and I. The topic of discussion was why we hadn't done any better for the executive committee. The meeting wasn't too harsh, they seemed fairly understanding. Later in the day we made several attempts to run the show, and had failures for the first four tries. The first time we nearly lost an arm on one of the figures. It had flipped behind him, and got caught in the lift as it went down. We received the new variable speed drive system for the raft. It's going to be a big job to get the thing installed. Maintenance is working on it. It has to be working in four days. I don't know if that's possible.

"Late tonight we finally ran a successful show with all the lifts and animation. Not too many people were there by the time we ran it – Norm Doerges and a few others. We called Wathel on the radio. He seemed happy. We needed it. Everybody clapped every time they saw something they hadn't seen before – all three set sevens coming up, Ben Franklin climbing the stairs. Ben worked because of the changes we'd made in the monitor cabinets. They even applauded when the flash powder went off; they didn't realize we were just faking it. They brought us all box lunches after we ran the successful show, and we took pictures of each other while we were eating."

1:40 AM, Friday, September 17, 1982

"Bob made good progress on the program today. He put in the feature that verifies the pressure sensors, but I think we may have a lot of trouble getting the lifts to run because of the inconsistency of the pressure sensors. Ed may be a little premature in asking us to put that into the program. I'm afraid it's going to keep us from getting anything done for quite a while. They're still making pressure sensor adjustments, and they're having a hard time doing it."

5:00 AM, Saturday, September 18, 1982

"I came in yesterday morning at about 10:00 AM after Melanie called. She was concerned over the pressure sensor adjustments. They hadn't finished and didn't look like they were going to any time soon. The situation persisted all day. In fact they're still working on them.

"I slept from midnight until 5:00 this morning in the upstairs gallery of the building, because I wasn't sure when they were going to need me."

1:34 PM, Saturday, September 18, 1982

"I've been in the building about 26 hours. They made good progress last night with the pressure sensors. Bob wrote the program so that it allows one sensor to drop out on a four-sensor lift, so the probability of eliminating failures is very good. I think that we'll be able to run successfully and still catch the failures that Ed is looking for. But it took about three days longer than it was supposed to.

"John Nacy of Reliance made good progress with the new variable speed drive for the raft. I saw him run it up and down slowly."

10:42 AM, Sunday, September 19, 1982

"At the moment I seem to be stuck behind an oak tree that's moving at about five miles per hour. The tree stopped at Mexico."

5:51 AM, Monday, September 20, 1982

"I've been here since 11:00 AM yesterday. We've been preparing the raft for vertical and horizontal motion, and the torch for vertical motion. I guess we embarrassed ourselves more than usual, because I said that it would be ready at noon. For all we could tell it was ready. We should have learned by now that nothing ever works. Even though it may have worked before, it never works when you need it.

"So it's 5:00 AM. We do have the torch going, but only as of about 4:00 AM. And we do have the raft moving horizontally, but only as of midnight. We haven't got the raft moving vertically yet. It wouldn't have been a problem, I suppose, to have taken that long to do the job, but we succeeded in keeping many people and much equipment tied up, expecting that we would be done shortly. An unending list of small problems kept cropping up. We tried out all the pieces but they just wouldn't come together into one functioning system. I cannot figure out how a system that was perfectly functional can stop working unless it's been tampered with.

"I sure hope we're finished soon. I can't tolerate too much more of this."

10:36 AM, Monday, September 20, 1982

"I'm finally able to leave the site. We had a fire this morning in the electrical box that contained the starter for the old raft motor. The thing caught on fire because some idiot put a fifteen-amp fuse where a 3/4 amp should have been. I put it out with a fire extinguisher. Those things really make a mess. I've got it all over me. To get to the fire I had to crawl back into an area that was only about 18 inches wide and about 15 feet off the ground. I was half asleep when it happened. It's a straight shot from now until opening, whatever hours it takes."

6:58 PM, Monday, September 20, 1982

"Talked to Derek. It seems that sleep was the key. The only reason that we set the place on fire this morning was that we were so sleepy that we shorted out the 110 volts."

7:15 AM, Tuesday, September 21, 1982

"Since I came in last night the raft has been programmed. The only problem is that we aren't getting the raft down fast enough. It's taking about twelve seconds, and it's supposed to take 10. I think that they're just going to have to live with it for now. I had an opportunity to show Conrad and Art around the building, and describe some of the kludges we've created in order to make the thing work. I emphasized how important it is that we get back in here to fix things up after opening. They seemed to understand.

"Cecil came by, and about that time we accidentally lowered the raft onto the large carriage. The command was issued from the animator's console by Davie too early. He just assumed that everything was interlocked."

* * *

Hydraulic and control problems with the incredibly complicated system continued to plague the attraction for the next week, and now there were real doubts about whether this centerpiece show would be ready for opening day. With the park already in soft opening, the pressure to run a successful show continued to mount. The first serious attempt to run a complete show was made September 27th, with just three days left before opening day. Linda describes it:

"My father was in town that week for the employee family preview, and every once in awhile we would drop by to see how American Adventure was doing, because we had heard that they were going to try to run their first show. Finally the radio call went out 'American Adventure 102.'

"We gathered in the holding area before the doors. Glenn came out and it was the only time I'd ever seen Glenn excited. He was jumping from foot to foot, so excited that he was beside himself. Steve wasn't up there. He was downstairs trying to get it all up and to keep it going. Nunis, Doerges, Zovich and Bongiorno were there. Everywhere I looked there were Disney people. Mickey was there, Judy, Gary Peterson, Rolando, June. I think just about everybody that could get in went. You could really feel the energy in that performance. I'd say that at least half the audience knew how complex what they were looking at was. It was as if all the lifts were being willed up by psychic energy. Towards the end of it when Walt Disney's face appeared on the screen, there was incredible applause. When it ended there was a standing ovation. It was just incredible."

Opening Day

At five o'clock in the morning on October 1, 1982, Glenn walked into the back door of American Adventure and clambered down the steps into the pit. He found Steve sitting on the floor by the control cabinet, staring glassy-eyed at the large carriage as it indexed its way through another show. Steve had been running the show all night, because they had discovered that if the hydraulic oil in the lift cylinders was allow to cool, the lifts were likely to hang up at some point during the complex sequence of moves.

Woozy but satisfied that he'd done his part, Steve staggered up the steps, wove his way back to Fort Wilderness. At their trailer, Linda was just getting ready to head to the site, to bring up all 10 of her pavilions for the park's first official day. Steve collapsed on the bed and slept through the opening day ceremonies.

But most of the engineers were there as Card Walker and the other Disney executives welcomed the first guests into "Walt Disney's greatest dream."

As it turned out, American Adventure never did manage to open on opening day. It would be several more days before the hydraulic system would operate reliably enough to generate enough confidence among the Operations team to warrant opening the front doors. The show ran sporadically during the coming weeks, finally hitting its stride in late October.

There were other problems with the newly opened park, too, including frequent downtimes in the Energy Pavilion ("Energy 101, Door B failed to open") and Spaceship Earth ("Spaceship Earth 101, Broken towbar").

There was also a shortage of places to sit, corrected by an emergency order for park benches. In fact, the park was so big that guests began to say EPCOT stood for "Every Person Comes Out Tired."

But on the whole, the park was a success. It boosted attendance at Disney World, and led to the multi-park pass, and achieved its goal of turning single day visits into weeklong stays. This, in turn, led to the development of thousands of additional hotel rooms, two more theme parks, and much more during the coming decades.

The final cost of EPCOT was somewhere around $1.2 Billion – a bit over the original budget of $400 Million! But EPCOT established the idea that Walt Disney World was a resort, a true destination, worthy of a weeklong stay, and not just an east coast Disneyland. It turned the outdoor entertainment division of the company into a major cash cow.

EPCOT was Card Walker's swan song; he would soon retire. During the coming decade, Disney would have a new leader, Michael Eisner, who would expand the company's business in all divisions, and all around the world.

After EPCOT opened, and contrary to the company's assurances, nearly every engineer in department 510 was laid off. But many of those same engineers would become consultants or be rehired to work on future projects.

Two decades later, although smaller, renamed and relocated, WED – now Walt Disney Imagineering – would still be populated by many of those same engineers.

They would travel the world, and work on even larger and more expensive projects than EPCOT Center.

But none of them would ever forget the experience of building a better mouse.

About the Authors

Steve Alcorn

Steve Alcorn is an entrepreneur, engineer, inventor, author and teacher best known for his involvement in the theme park industry.

After an early career in the personal computer and music businesses, in 1982 he joined Walt Disney Imagineering (then known as WED Enterprises) as a consultant, where he worked on the electronic systems for EPCOT Center. During his two years with Imagineering he designed show control systems for The American Adventure, wrote the operating system used in the parkwide monitoring system, and became Imagineering's first Systems Engineer.

In 1986 he founded Alcorn McBride Inc. The company's show control, audio, video, and lighting equipment is used in most major theme park attractions around the world.

Mr. Alcorn is the author of a dozen novels and non-fiction books available at themeperks.com. Through wrtingacademy.com he has taught more than 40,000 students how to structure their writing.

He also teaches a survey class in Theme Park Engineering at themeparkengineering.com

David Green

David Paul Green is president and COO of Los Angeles-based lighting design firm Visual Terrain, Inc. After starting off in themed entertainment at WED Enterprises (now Walt Disney Imagineering), working on EPCOT, Disneyland, and Tokyo Disneyland, David went on to work with Walt Disney Feature Animation, Walt Disney Studios, Disney TeleVentures, and a secret division of Disney.com. As principal at consulting firm Monteverdi Creative, David was inventor or co-inventor on nine U.S. Patents for innovations in digital TV user interface design for DIRECTV.

David has written for InPark Magazine, Lighting & Sound America, and others. His photography has been featured in 14 exhibits since 2009. Six of his images are in the permanent collection of the California African American Museum, and were featured in the catalog and exhibit, "Allensworth: A Place. A People. A Story," and later in "Taking Place: Selections from the Permanent Collection" exhibit.

An alumnus of Cal State University, Northridge, David holds a Masters of Arts in Writing, and Bachelors Degrees in Journalism and English.

David lives in Santa Clarita with his wife, Lisa Passamonte Green.

Made in the USA
Columbia, SC
01 December 2024

48167723R00087